Also by the same Author

Salute Goliath!

THE GREAT CON

Disastrous Effects of Bible Double-Speak

by

M. Kennedy

Published in 1999 by MARION BOOKS
P.O. Box 28207
EDINBURGH
EH9 1WL
UK

Copyright M.Kennedy, 1999

ISBN 0-9536291-1-2

Printed and bound in the UK by THE PRINT CONSULTANCY
0131 667 5549

CONTENTS

THE GREAT CON

INTRODUCTION

The people in the pews are uncomfortable. It is not hard seats that are making them so: the discomfort is moral and spiritual, not physical. The message of much of the Bible is immoral, and their moral sense is grieved. Many have been so upset by the message that they have left the Church. Others attend services sometimes, and just hope that *that* day there will be no Old Testament readings of battles and killings, which give the credit to God.

It is not any individual minister who is to blame for this situation. It is the message of Christianity, handed down through the generations. This message includes the central tenets of Judaism, as spelled out in the Old Testament, which are that God made a covenant with Abraham, of special blessings, countless descendants and a Land, in return for obedience. Obedience turned out to be slaughtering the inhabitants of all coveted territory, instead of adherence to the Moral Code pretended. *This* is the dilemma for Christians, causing their discomfort in the pew: how much longer can they go on accepting that this was, indeed, of God?

CHAPTER 1

A GOD FOR EVERYONE

"The Bible says..."
(Quoted by thousands of religious people to justify the outrageous statement they are about to make.)

If God gave away my house, I would not like him, I wouldn't love him, and neither would I worship him. Nor would I if he gave away my land, be it my garden (if I *had* one) or Scotland.

Why, then, should I worship a God who did that to anyone else? It would not be logical to do so, and would clearly indicate that I had double standards, and did not live by the motto, "Do as you would be done by", which is a good yardstick of morality - indeed, it is the best one.

But those double standards are what the Church has been teaching as Christianity down the ages. It is obvious to little children that, if God is not for everyone, he is not a God worth having. A three-year-old child can tell you that; one told me. It is a travesty of God to say he is *for* some, and *not for* others: it is blasphemy!

Yet the Church has been teaching this travesty and this blasphemy for nearly two thousand years. Why? Because, instead of working out the implications of Jesus' life, death and teaching, *apart* from Judaism - which rejected him, and which he largely rejected - Christian teachers have gone on reiterating the old jargon and concepts, which the earliest Christians, who were, of course, Jews, passed on to them. It was entirely appropriate for those first Christians to see Jesus as the fulfilment of their religion; indeed, the Church preaches him as fulfilling the unfulfilled part of *all* religions, therefore, the fulfilment of them *all*, but that does not mean that it takes the scriptures of them all as its own. Jesus was a Jew, preaching mainly to Jews. His teaching was bound to be couched in terms of the Jewish Law, in which he had been educated, and which was familiar to his hearers, even though he turned much of it on its head. Moreover, all the writers of the New Testament, except Luke, were Jews, and wrote in terms of their own religious traditions and upbringing, naturally.

But Judaism was not a religion for all mankind. It was for one select line of one man, Abraham - not even for all his offspring! A people chosen by God to

3

be specially blessed and protected, and, worst of all, told they must *kill* other nations and take their lands, *may* sound all right if you belong to the chosen tribe (*if* you cannot put yourself in the others persons' shoes, and see, of course, that it is *wrong*) but it should *never* sound all right to anyone else! Of course, it does not sound right, either, to any right-thinking person in the group selected for the special prize, as it *did* not to the Hebrew nation itself - until their leader got rid of all the opposition, and terrorised the rest into subjection - as we shall see.

Christianity has not known what to make of the Old Testament, yet, illogically and ridiculously, it has taught the Old Testament, as well as the New, as Holy Scripture, the very Word, and words, of God, God-breathed, God-inspired, every word relevant to everyone! On the one hand, the Church says this is the Word of God, whilst on the other hand, it ignores much of it, where it is too mysterious, or embarrassing, or otherwise inconvenient. The rabbis complain, "Christians pick and choose what they want of the Old Testament". Precisely! And that is one thing you cannot logically do: either the *whole* of it is The Word of God, or *none* of it is. It cannot be that *some* bits are, and some bits are not - for which *would* be, and which *wouldn't*?

The Word of God cannot be written in books, nor yet on Tablets of Stone! The Word of God can only be our *conscience*, nothing else. It can only be that knowledge within, that conviction that we should always treat others well, because we would like them to treat *us* well. We have this amazing and mysterious faculty in us, for recognising and judging right and wrong. Even more to the point - it is more reliable than all the religious, social and moral codes put together, for *they* can lead us into terrible deeds, but conscience, where it is undamaged by indoctrination, or by mental illness, never does.

Those who claim to know the *mind* of God, and have the very *words* of God, should be treated with great scepticism and suspicion - and if their words and actions do not coincide with what your conscience tells you is right, they should be treated with disdain. Traditionally such claimants have expected, even demanded, veneration and adulation, and have received it. Such leaders are to be feared. They are after one thing - power. Check out everything they tell you with your conscience. *You* have as much access to God as they. Think about it!

Many Native Americans knew this, and thus rightly discerned the poor quality of what Christian missionaries arrogantly came offering them, calling it the

4

very Truth of God. Wonderfully, the reply by Chief Seneca, in 1805, declining to have a certain Mr. Cram among them, has been preserved. It shows clearly a level of wisdom, and an ability to discern true spirituality, so superior to that of the self-styled evangelists as to be beyond their ken.

Here are some of the Chief's words:

"You say that you are right, and we are lost. How do we know this to be true? We understand that your religion is written in a book. If it was intended for us, as well as you, why has not the Great Spirit given to us - and not only to us, but to our forefathers, the knowledge of that book, with the means of understanding it rightly? We only know what you tell us about it. How shall we know when to believe, being so often deceived by the white people? ... If there is but one religion, why do you white people differ so much about it? Why not all agree, as you can all read the book? ... We do not wish to destroy *your* religion or take it from you; we only want to enjoy our own... We have been told that you have been preaching to the white people in this place... We will wait a little while and see what effects your preaching has on them. If we find it does them good, makes them honest and less disposed to cheat Indians, we will consider again what you have said."

The refusal of Cram to shake hands with the Natives, saying, "There is no fellowship between the religion of God and the Devil", tells us all we need to know of his brand of Christianity!

How right the indigenous people were to refuse the religion of this book, for in it they would have read of a nightmare like their own, being visited upon *another* people by those who claimed to have "the light" - for the book tells of the oh-so-innocent-sounding *Children* of Israel inflicting an unholy terror and genocide on an indigenous people for a land they wanted. Some Christian Bibles and books even call the mass-murder, rape and plunder in Canaan "Holy War"! Our consciences tell us otherwise!

What, then, is the religion of this book that Christian missionaries have been peddling all over the world? They would like us to believe it is a moral and spiritual message - and in some parts it is - but it has *immoral* and *unspiritual* foundations, which call the whole religion into question. Its immoral and unspiritual foundations need to be re-examined by the Church, and not disregarded any longer. *The biggest con in history* must be exposed for what it is - a *trick*, claiming that God gave one group of people the right to kill others and take their lands. The Church has believed and taught this lie, calling it the Old Testament, or Covenant.

There never *could* have been such a covenant with God. Apart from it being unsubstantiable, the immorality of it makes it untenable! It is not good enough to say God is a God of love, yet turned perfectly normal people into mass-murderers because he did not like the religion of those who became their victims. Is butchering people, down to the smallest new-born baby a superior religion to idol-worship? Not in *my* book! It is high time for the Church to face up to this self-evident truth.

The Christian Bible, source of the Church's erroneous doctrines, has two main parts, the Old Testament and the New Testament, each named according to its belief in the two covenants, one between God and Abraham, and one between Jesus and his followers. Each of the two parts is a collection of smaller books, some of them very short. The Old Testament is one of the holy books of Judaism, and pre-dates Jesus of Nazareth. The New Testament deals with Jesus, and the founding of the Christian Church.

The first five books, Genesis to Deuteronomy, attributed to Moses by the Jews, are called by them, The Law, or Torah. Christian scholars call those books, collectively, the Pentateuch. This is the section that is read week by week, over a year, in the synagogues, and rejoiced over, when the reading has been completed and restarted, at the Festival of Simchat Torah. It is also the part of the Bible that Jewish men touch and kiss with their prayer shawls, in the synagogue, symbolising how precious God's Law is to them. Do they notice all the promises of cursing by God, if they are unfaithful, that they find it so sweet, I wonder? There are many bitter words, and there is much harshness in those books.

Next comes the History section - Joshua to Nehemiah, although the history, in fact, begins in Genesis Chapter 12, with the story of Abraham, whom scholars estimate lived @ 1800 BC. The Exodus from Egypt is recounted in the book of that name, with the building of the Tabernacle in the desert, on the way to Canaan. The tyranny of the religious rulers, and the terrorising of the people by them through harsh punishments, are told there, along with the conquest of the indigenous people, and the seizing of their land, under the judges and kings. Then comes the defeat of the northern kingdom, Israel, by Assyria, when the Hebrew population was transferred to other conquered territory, and replaced with another conquered people, presumably with the purpose of making revolt less likely. Later, the southern kingdom, Judah, was conquered by Babylon, and most of its population taken there, in a period known as The Exile. When Babylon, in turn, was conquered by Cyrus of Persia, in 539 BC, the captives were allowed home.

After that come The Writings - Esther to Song of Solomon - stories, poems, songs, proverbs and sermons: a very disparate collection.

The Prophets comprise the last section of the Old Testament - Isaiah to Malachi. Their message has a very different ring from the ritualistic religion of the Torah. They call for a religion of the *heart* - one of *justice* and *kindness*, not of sacrifices and outward show. This part of the Old Testament is much more in keeping with the teaching of Jesus. No wonder religious Jews do not seem to vererate their Prophecy as much as their Law!

After the return from the Exile in Babylon, there is a gap of about four hundred years, until the birth of Christ, and the beginning of the New Testament. The first four books are the "gospels" of Matthew, Mark, Luke and John, which are the record of Jesus' life and teaching. Next comes the book of Acts, which tells of the Early Church. Thereafter, come letters to individuals and churches, most of them written by the Apostle Paul. Last of all, there is a book of recorded visions, called Revelation. This book does not inspire many sermons, or much study, in the established churches, but is much studied, and speculated on by modern Bible-based religions and cults.

There are also fourteen books, collectively called The Apocrypha, which are not part of the Jewish or Protestant Bibles, but were included in some early Christian Bibles, and are included in the Roman Catholic Bible. Most of the Apocrypha is similar to various books of the Bible, its authors probably having used material from the same sources as the Bible authors.

This is a very rough outline of the books of the Christian Bible. What they teach, and how they are misinterpreted, misunderstood and misused, I will deal with in subsequent chapters.

CHAPTER 2

THE DOUBLE-SPEAK OF THE OLD TESTAMENT

"Kill them all. Make no treaties with them. Show them no mercy."
(Deuteronomy 7 v 2)
"He (God) is kind and merciful." (Joel 2 v 13)

The Christian Holy Book, the Bible, is very confusing. No wonder - it was not written as a book at all, but is a collection of many documents, some of which are themselves collections of tales, like the first eleven chapters of Genesis. These chapters, so scholars tell us, are an anthology of very ancient stories - myths of oral tradition, from different areas of the Middle East, passed down many generations, before they ever came to be written down. However, *this* is not the cause of the confusion. The confusion comes about because two *contrary* pictures of God are given: one presents God as kind, loving, merciful and moral, whilst the other presents a God who is a murderous monster. When we realise this, we can begin to sort out the confusion, but *until this confusion is admitted and faced up to,* we are floundering, trying to make sense out of nonsense! The real trouble in Christianity is that, instead of admitting there are two mutually exclusive pictures of God in the Bible, and saying one of these is wrong, it tries to fuse the two irreconcilable characters into one, and say, "This is God, and he is good"! And *this* is a futile exercise!

The confusion is carried on into the New Testament, naturally enough, because the first Christians had been brought up in the Jewish tradition of interpreting the monster God of peevishness, partisanship and harsh punishments, as their God, who loved morality, and who gave them The Ten Commandments. Christian teachers down the ages have failed to come to terms with the contradiction there. They have tried to teach that the Bible has *no* contradictions, or that, whatever inconsistencies there are are small, and do not matter. They are *not* small, and they *do* matter: they were a matter of life and death to the people of the Old Testament. They have continued to be so down the generations, and they are still a matter of life and death to the people of the Middle East today.

Christians are sick of the fudging of this issue. They know there is something radically wrong with the teaching handed down. They are disgusted by the passing off of mass-murderers of the Old Testament as heroes in the New, and they are leaving the Church in droves. Many of them would like to return, for they love Jesus and most of his teaching, yet, when they attend a service of worship, they come away feeling strangely upset, and do not know why. Every Christian probably senses something wrong with the message, and with the portrayal of God.

The Church has tried to say that the message of the Bible is a unity, namely, God's plan of redemption for sinful man (and woman). It tries to teach that the only thing wrong is our sin. The official teaching does not admit that there is anything inconsistent or wrong with the picture of God that Church doctrines give. Some resourceful people say that it all makes sense if you put the Bible into *chronological order*, and see a progressively improving picture of God. This *might* be an acceptable way of looking at it, if the doctrines arising from the *unimproved* picture were discarded - but they are not! Christianity *still* teaches that God deliberately drowned nearly everything and everyone in a great flood, and that he was right to do so! It *still* teaches that God inspired genocide, and was right to do so. It is pitiful to think of the contortions of morality, psychology and logic required to make these, and other tales from the Old Testament say, "God is love" - yet the Church does these contortions!

Other theologians say, "If only people would see that the Bible history was not written down at the time it tells about, but much later - hundreds of years later - they would realise that it is an *idealised account,* making the conquest of Canaan, for example, sound much more glorious, and more complete, than it actually was, for we know that the Canaanites were not entirely wiped out."

A few things can be said about *this* view. Firstly - whether the history is embroidered to make it sound that the attacks on the Canaanites were always more successful, and more complete than they really were, makes no difference to the fact that they were understood to be instigated by *God*, and that they were unprovoked by those who were attacked. Something very violent happened to the indigenous people, for, in the end, the land *did* pass into the hands of the invaders.

Secondly, the scholars' theory that the writers of the Bible record *wished for* more deaths than there actually were, *betrays an ungodly barbarism* in them, whereas, with the land in their possession, and with the lapse of years, they *could* have been magnanimous, and shown a little sympathy for those so cruelly put down! But there is *no* trace of any compassion for the victims of their merciless aggression, even all these years later. So much for the Christian Fundamentalists' view that the writers were vehicles of the Holy Spirit, writing down what God inspired!

Thirdly, the values are upside down: for "glorious conquest" read "barbaric invasion" - it makes much more sense. And lastly, it would appear that, from any interpretation but the *last* one, for the relief we might feel that *some* Canaanites survived, we cannot say, "Thank God"!

Let me spell out here, then, what is wrong with the picture of God in the Old Testament. It teaches that God chose *one* nation, and told them to murder others and take their lands. It tries to say this is right and good, since it was God who willed it. It says that the written record of it is God's Word, which "is a light to our feet, and a lamp unto our path". Thus we can learn that if we believe we are God's people, we have an example to follow of "kill and take", for whatever *we* want is what God wants! This is the circular logic that operates in the context of the Bible.

The Christian Church tries hard not to see it this way. It says, "God *had* to choose a nation for *Christ* to be born into, and that happened to be the Hebrew nation". It fails to see that *whatever* nation Christ was born into must not be above criticism. *Any* nation that decides to kill off others *must* be criticized, and certainly must *not* be allowed to get away with genocide saying, "God told us to do it"! Far from being believed, it should be firmly told, "God would not do that!"

Not only has the Church down the ages failed to say this, it has failed to see this self-evident *truth,* and all its branches have adopted, and incorporated into their teaching, the insupportable doctrines of The Chosen People and The Promised Land. Those are the ideas involved in The Old Covenant.

Even if, for argument's sake, we say that *all* nations, long ago, won their territory by force, and acted savagely - *no* other nation waged war, pillage, rape and genocide *in the name of its God,* and had its religion respected. Alexander the Great gave the credit for his victories and his massacres to his God, but that failed to convince the world that his must therefore be a great religion. Similarly, the Aztecs slaughtered people daily to sacrifice to their God, but we do not think they had anything to teach the world where religion is concerned. We see them as barbarous, and rightly so; murderers have *nothing* to teach others in the realms of morality or religion!

But *not* all ancient nations slaughtered those they invaded. When the two kingdoms of Israel and Judah were invaded, the conquerors did *not* put their subjugated populations to death. Huge numbers were moved to other places, *but they were allowed to live.* Daniel and Esther got on very well in their new countries, as the books of their names testify, evidence in Hebrew writings, that they were in receipt of much better treatment than they ever meted out to the people they vilified. Hebrew survivors and their progeny were allowed back to Judah, as the Books of Ezra and Nehemiah tell.

The other thing that is wrong with the Christian implementation of this doctrine of a Chosen People being given the land of others, is the blind acceptance of the version of the story given by the usurpers. Bias goes unquestioned! This is so intellectually unsound as to be laughable, were it not such a serious matter. Even *if* God had told the Israelites to kill the Canaanites and take their land, morally speaking *it should put us off God, not* put us on the side of the killers! Traditional Christian teaching is that the Old Testament is a book about morality, and depicts a moral God, because it contains The Ten Commandments. It might mention in passing that Babylon, the region the patriarch Abraham came from, and Egypt, where Moses had been brought up, had similar moral codes, predating that of the Israelites, but it is hardly suggested, in sermons, that the Israelites' decalogue was modelled on those other codes. Why not? It is also entirely glossed over that the doctrine of a Chosen People and a Promised Land contradicts *every* moral code, because implementing such a doctrine involves the breaking of the spirit of it by both sides - by God's, as well as the nation's.

In fact, The Ten Commandments are a red herring. They function as a distraction from what is really going on in the religion. They are there to make people *believe* there is morality where there is *not*! The religion of the Old Testament is not about keeping The Ten Commandments, but about *breaking* them. What the religion is *really* about is seizing a land and pretending God sanctioned it. The religion is *greed* and *genocide*, defying all known morality!

"Thou shalt not covet" is one of the commandments, but it was Abraham's covetous eyes and heart, that started off the process whereby a longing became a dream, and the dream was passed down the generations, that God would give certain of his many descendants a land he saw and liked, a land where he had arrived as a foreigner, and had been treated well by its hospitable inhabitants, a land he would like for himself.

This *dream* became their religion. When life became hard for them in Egypt, a country they *chose* to go to - no one forced them - Moses set out to take them to the land of their dreams. The Ten Commandments were a good smoke-screen for the immorality upon which the implementation of the dream depended. Famous for *delivering* them, he should also be famous for *breaking* them! He systematically broke them *all*.

1   *Have no gods but me.*
Far from being the meek man he was described to be, in Numbers 12 v 3, Moses' God was *power*. Neither God's laws (as he claimed they were) nor the people's wish for another leader, would he allow to get in his way.
(Numbers 16 is a victor's version of one rebellion against him.)

2   *Do not worship graven images.*
He delivered tablets of stone, engraved by himself, after he, in a tantrum, broke the ones he claimed *God* engraved! These became like an idol, carried into battle, with death mysteriously visited upon anyone who looked inside the Covenant Box, and even on one helpful man, whose only crime was to put out a steadying hand to stop it falling off the cart going over uneven ground!
(1 Samuel 6, and 2 Sam 6)

3   *Do not blaspheme.*
It is the ultimate blasphemy to say God wants murder, massacre, rape and pillage.

4   *Keep the Sabbath Day holy.*
Turning the population into killers was evidently seen as a holier way of keeping the Sabbath than collecting firewood was. (Num 15 v 32-36)

5   *Honour your parents.*
Moses' parents-in-law were Midianite, and Moses oversaw the massacre of that nation. (Num 31)

6   *Do not kill.*
Moses killed an Egyptian before his religious life started. Thereafter he was responsible for the deaths of many thousands of his own people, as well as the hundreds of thousands, perhaps millions, of others.

7   *Do not commit adultery.*
The female virgins of Midian, perhaps down to the smallest baby girl, were kept alive to be the sexual playthings of the Israelite men. (Num 31)

8   *Do not steal.*
Before leaving Egypt, the Israelites were told to borrow gold and silver jewellery from the Egyptians - but they did not intend to pay it back (Exodus 12 v 35). This was stealing. Everything in Canaan was also stolen by them.

9   *Do not tell lies.*
The worst lie is to say good is evil, and evil is good.

10   *Do not covet what belongs to others.*
Moses very deliberately got the Israelites to covet everything the Canaanites had, as part of his motivating strategy. (Deuteronomy 6 v 11)

Thus, the first part of the Bible is about stealing the Land of Canaan. No one in their right mind could say that this was a godly thing to do. God should/ could/would have given "his chosen" an empty land, if he was so keen for them to have one - or made the people there change their minds about living there, and conveniently leave. But, no - Christian professors have traditionally tried to tell us this was all God's doing. It beggars belief!

The prophets, however, try to put some morality into the picture. They realise something is radically wrong with the religion, and rightly diagnose that it is its lack of morality - it is too concerned with observing certain rituals, doing things in a prescribed way, performing the correct sacrifices... The prophets are united in calling for justice and mercy for the poor. Some, like Isaiah, Hosea and Amos, go so far as to say the sacrifices *were never instituted by God* (Isaiah 1 v 11, Hosea 6 v 6, Amos 5 v 25).

Jesus, although he drove the merchants and moneylenders out of the Temple in Jerusalem (Matthew 21 v 12), did not seem to criticise the sacrificial system. Certainly, he taught that the heart had to be right, that sacrifices without love were hypocrisy, and he championned the Sinner class, those who were uninterested in the sacrificial system and the keeping of strict rules for living - the Law.

Christian teachers, however, teach the unacceptable - that the seizure of Canaan, and the genocide of the Canaanites was part of God's plan for the redemption of the world, and *redeemed from the Devil, at that* ! This means that because of the actions of two mythical figures (Adam and Eve), the world needed to be bought back from Satan (a "fallen" *angel*!), and so God chose a nation for his Son to be born into. But before he could be born into it, the nation had to learn to be mass murderers, and annihilate other nations, and thus his Son could save the doomed world! See?

Let us hope Christian theologians will now put their minds to improving this ludicrous theology. The war ethic in Christianity has brought disgrace on it in the eyes of the world, and, more than anything else, brought it into disrepute. This is what inspired the unjustifiable Crusades of the Middle Ages. It inspired the unjustifiable attacks on defenceless people in far-flung places east and west, paving the way for colonization and oppression of all kinds, even annihilation of races, deliberately carried out by those who thought they were superior to others, but were *not* - justified by the religion of a book they described as "holy", or, at least, by the religion of *part* of that book. They could never have justified such conduct from what Jesus taught.

There is, nevertheless, double-speak in the New Testament, also, which is the subject of the next chapter.

CHAPTER 3

DICHOTOMY IN THE NEW TESTAMENT

"I did not come to destroy the Law, but to fulfil it." (Matthew 5 v 17-18)

THE OLD LAW OF EXCLUSION

The words of Jesus, quoted above, pose a problem for Christians, which is, "What Law did he mean?" Did he mean only The Ten Commandments, or did he mean the whole Jewish Law, as set out in the Torah? If he meant the Torah, does this mean he approved of all six hundred and thirteen laws, with severe penalties for minor infringements, often *death,* for little non-sins like collecting firewood on the Sabbath? Does it mean he was in favour of all the laws of diet, of washing, of punishments, of sacrifices, of exclusions of people deemed to be unacceptable to God...?
"No one who has had his genitals cut off may be included in the Lord's people. No one born illegitimate, nor his descendants, even to the tenth generation, shall be included. No Ammonite nor Moabite..." (Deut 23)

Such exclusions give God a bad name. No right-thinking person would believe that God approved of keeping *anyone* out of the Church - and Israel is the Church in the Old Testament, according to Christian doctrine - especially the downtrodden, the despised, those who had suffered at the hands of others. Those, indeed, were the very ones cited as loved by God in the teaching of Jesus (Matt 5). And *none* of us was able to choose whether we were born legitimate or not!

THE NEW LAW OF *INCLUSION* AND LOVE

Of course Jesus did not aim to fulfil that pitiless and exclusive idea of "law" in the Torah. We see this by the things he did, as well as by the things he taught, for he constantly and deliberately *broke* the Sabbath laws by healing the sick and disabled, by "grinding" corn between his fingers... He did not wash his hands, in the way laid down, before eating. He chose friends from the class that was outside the Law, the Sinners. He made despised people, and foreigners, heroes in his parables. He praised the faith of a Roman Centurion above anything he found in Israel. Those reckoned to be unloved by God under the old Law, the poor, the sick, the disabled, are explicitly referred to as loved by God in his teaching.

Jesus deliberately broke laws which were nothing to do with honouring God, but were all to do with the power wielded by religious leaders. He did believe in keeping sensible laws, even if they were unpopular, like paying taxes to Caesar. He was concerned to show that laws were a rough and ready guide to the *real law*, which should operate in our hearts - the law of *love*. If we let love rule in our hearts, it would eliminate hatred and anger from our lives. This would transform individual and national life. He taught that the righteousness of his followers must exceed that of the Scribes and Pharisees: they *appeared* to be righteous, correct, law-abiding. It was outward show, Jesus said, for their hearts were hard. They lacked love, and it was *love* that counted with God. Jesus lived and died for *that* law. Without love, the law is a poor thing, even a fearsome thing. Jesus showed how precepts of love, and a quickened conscience transformed the law, even transcended it. The law of Moses was *not* the one Jesus was concerned to fulfil, but the law of love.

The Mosaic Law failed to fulfil its own spirit, stated in Leviticus 19 v 18 - "Love thy neighbour as thyself". The Jewish Law was harsh on its own people, let alone Gentiles (foreigners), who were generally despised, as they were assumed to worship inferior gods. One such was the hero of the parable of The Good Samaritan (Luke 10). Not only that, but the parable demonstrated that the code of conduct operating in the Samaritan's life, based on *love*, was superior to the religious law operating in the lives of the priest and Levite. Not only did their law allow them to pass by the injured traveller, and not help, but passing by was almost mandatory, for to have helped him would have made them "unclean", unfit for their stint of duty in the Temple, to which they were probably on their way. Loving his neighbour was shown to operate in the life of the Samaritan, who did *not* have the law that commanded it, whilst the two who *had* that law passed by, leaving their neighbour for dead, or to die.

Does Jesus confirm or abolish the Law of the Torah? He transcends it, showing that all laws need to be backed by a spirit of *love*.

THE SCRIPTURES TELL OF ME (John 5 v 39)

Another reference to the Law, which perplexes Christians, is that in Luke 24 v 44, "...all things must be fulfilled, which were written in the Law of Moses, and in the prophets, and in the Psalms, concerning me."

What on Earth are those references to him in the law, the prophets, and the Psalms? Christian sermons abound in finding them, and very contrived, and unlikely, some of the claims seem to me. I can only think that the imperfect Law of Moses, lacking as it is in love, is fulfilled (=complemented) in Jesus' teaching and example of love.

"The messianic secret" - Jesus' request to the people he healed at the beginning of his ministry, that they do not tell anyone who he was (the Messiah), could only have been for the reason that he wanted time to spread his new teaching before he was killed - as he understood, from his own study of the scriptures, would be the inevitable conclusion of his words and actions. The *imperfection* in the Law would bring this about. It would put him to death for blasphemy *because it, itself was blasphemous,* portraying a harsh God, who demanded animal sacrifices, and tyrannised individuals through his priests. Well, if it demanded sacrifices, Jesus demonstrated that he fulfilled that, too. Luke 22 v 16 shows us that he saw his death as the fulfilment of the Passover Feast. He saw himself as the sacrificial lamb, an offering for sin, but the final one, *the fulfilment.* The offering of himself, since it was ordered by the Chief Priests, fulfilled their law better than they knew, for it fulfilled their blasphemous law, and a better one was coming to replace it, a law of brotherly love, of equality of all people, of care, concern, and justice for all, ruling in people's hearts. *This* law, if ever implemented, would transform the world!

THE CONFUSION BEGINS

But soon this radical new message was hijacked into just another religion, with priests, fancy costumes and fancy rituals, ornamentation, elaboration and pomp. *What a pity!* In this new religion of pretty costumes, pictures, rites, holy places and ceremonies, the radical new message became obscured. The New became like the Old, in more ways than one.

The two radically different messages of the Old and New Testaments became deliberately merged, instead of being kept separate and distinct. The Old Testament became accepted as *foreshadowing Christ*, instead of being seen as falling short, and *requiring Christ.* The New Testament came to be seen as *requiring* the Old, in order to be valid, instead of being understood as overriding and *invalidating* the Old, which could never bring glory to God, for all its pretentions to grandeur.

THE TRADITIONS OF MEN

"Why do you transgress the commandment of God by your tradition?" (Matthew 15 v 3)

The dichotomy of Jesus' teaching is that, whilst he turned the traditional teaching of Judaism on its head, deliberately breaking some of its less important laws, in order to reveal the true spirit, both of that law, as it was, and the law, *as it should be* - by so doing he was not abolishing it, but fulfilling it, in a way never before dreamt of. Fulfil it by *breaking* it? Yes - because the Judaistic Law broke the spirit of the very law it claimed to uphold. We have all seen examples in our lives of how applying rigorously the letter of the law can break the spirit of it.

Furthermore, The Ten Commandments were broken by additions to laws, or ways round having to keep them. One of these was instanced by Jesus in Matthew 15: the Law of Corban (a vow to give money to the Temple) was sometimes used as an excuse not to help out needy parents. This was breaking the Fifth Commandment.

Even more serious was this example. "Thou shalt not kill" was broken by the death penalty being used for many paltry crimes, and was more prevalent for women than for men. In John 8, Jesus refused to support the call for the death penalty for the woman "taken in adultery". Notice, there was no call for capital punishment for the man. Where was he? Nowhere to be seen!

Nor was the official religious policy of treating foreigners well *ever* thought of as applying to the Canaanites. "Thou *shalt* kill" was the policy for them!

The laws which Jesus broke were not wholesome laws, which every society needs for the protection of individuals and groups, but the silly rules and regulations which made the law an ass.

THE MESSIAH

"Prophets foretold him, infant of wonder", we sing at Christmas. The rabbis say that Christians take Old Testament texts and misapply them to Jesus - that a text such as Isaiah 7 v 14, "a virgin shall conceive, and shall bear a son", does not at all mean what Christians say it does, but was referring to a better time coming soon to the people the prophet was addressing. Similarly, they claim that the "suffering servant" prophecies of Chapter 42 and following, refer to the Jewish nation. The Gospel writer, Matthew, goes somewhat over the top in his zeal of finding prophecies that Jesus allegedly fulfilled, as when he applies Hosea 11 v 1 to Jesus: "Out of Egypt have I called my son", Matt 2 v 15.

Jesus himself seemed deliberately to set about fulfilling the prophecy in Zechariah 9 v 9, "Behold, thy king cometh unto thee; he is just, and having salvation; lowly, and riding upon an ass, upon a colt, the foal of an ass" - for we read that he sent his disciples to a certain house, with instructions for borrowing someone's colt, upon which he rode into Jerusalem the Sunday before his death, when the crowd waved palm branches, and shouted, "Hosanna", the day the Church celebrates as Palm Sunday (Luke 19 v 30). This was a claim to messiahship on his part.

Jesus, doubtless, saw himself as the fulfilment of Psalm 23, "The Lord is my shepherd", when he made statements such as, "I am the Good Shepherd", and when he told his parable of The Lost Sheep (Luke 15). Certainly, the Church interprets many lines in the Psalms as referring to him, as 24 v 9, "Lift up your heads, O ye gates... and the *King of glory* shall come in."

Altogether, then, Jesus saw himself as the Messiah (The Anointed One), the long-awaited leader of Judaism, with the various strands of the Old Testament referring to him - the Law (with the qualification that the law mean a moral code, and not arbitrary man-made rules), the Prophets, and the Psalms.

Judaism rejects Jesus' claim to messiahship, saying that no one who broke the Sabbath laws could possibly be the Messiah. Jesus seems to have been particularly enthusiastic about breaking the Sabbath laws, performing his miracles and healings on the Sabbath. Of course, the Sabbath was the only time when people were free from work, and able to go and listen to his teaching. He also showed great disrespect to the religious leaders, calling them "hypocrites", "whited sepulchres", "blind guides", and "sons of Hell"! But he was keen on befriending Sinners, that lower class, despised in the religion, which, understandably, was not much interested in taking its rituals seriously.

Death on a cross was the very antithesis of the kind of death fit for the Messiah: the cross was for the Sinner class. This death is exactly what Christians appreciate in a Saviour: in his death Jesus is identifying completely with Sinners - the despised, the rejected.   Thus, the Cross became a very suitable symbol for Christianity, "to the Jews a stumblingblock, and unto the Greeks foolishness, but unto them which are called, both Jews and Greeks, Christ, the power of God, and the wisdom of God" (1 Corinthians 1 v 23-24).

CHAPTER 4

ABRAHAM

"The one we treated as a brother is now our enemy." Iroquois story

A Native American, Joseph Bruchac, tells the story from Iroquois folklore of a boy called Hahjanoh, who found a two-headed snake. It was small and starving, but he took it home, fed and cared for it. It grew to be big and beautiful. The whole village admired it, and approved of the boy's kindness in saving it and looking after it.

But the story is about treachery, for one day the snake began to terrorise the village, eating the children. When Hahjanoh confronted the snake, he asked, "How could you betray us? We treated you as a brother. Now you want to destroy us all."

This story is all too tragically analogous of what happened to the Native Americans at the hands of the European settlers, whom many tribes befriended, and whose lives they saved, in the early years of invasion: the first settlements grew into a monster which decimated their population, and destroyed their culture.

The story of Abraham is, likewise, a story of treachery. Treated well by everyone in Canaan, he has a covetous dream, which involves destroying those who treated him as a brother.

Abraham could be the prototype of the traveller with his "traveller's tales". Indeed, his tales give extra meaning to the word "adulterated" as he journeys abroad, twice passing off his wife as his sister, and marrying her to two kings - one the Pharaoh of Egypt - for fear of meeting characters as devious as he is (Genesis 12 v 19; 20 v 6)!

But no one he meets is as devious as he! On his travels he meets friendly people, innocents, who have not his propensity for guile. They take him at face value, believing what he says, treating him with respect, assuming he is a man of his word. Indeed, they shower him with gifts - until they discover what a fraud he is!

His hosts are shocked at his gratuitous lies. No one was going to kill him in order to take his wife from him. The wicked thought was in his own mind, and no one else's. King Abimelech and the Pharaoh are only too relieved to have discovered in time that Sara is a married woman. They did not wish to have on their consciences the sin of taking another man's wife. The Pharaoh throws Abraham out of Egypt, as he deserves (Gen 12 v 20). King Abimelech, generous to a fault, lets him stay on in southern Canaan (Gen 20 v 15).

Travelling he may be, but he is not a nomad. He left his home with the express idea of *settling* somewhere. He eyes up all the territory he passes through, for possible future settlement. He will recognise the land when he sees it, for it will be a "Land Flowing With Milk And Honey". He soon arrives at the fertile land he has in mind. It is Canaan.

Let us be clear at the outset: Abraham found no enemies in Canaan. Travelling south-east from Haran, his home, he met amiable, peaceful people, who treated him well - the kind of people he envisaged his descendants could defeat in battle, and acquire their territory. Why not take Egypt also? After all, he wanted most of the other lands he passed through. Presumably, Egypt's army looked too strong for him to imagine his descendants defeating it, and it was not included in his territorial ambitions. Later, this omission was explained as gratitude to the Egyptians for having given sanctuary to the Israelites during the famous seven year famine, and afterwards for four hundred and thirty years. *Why no similar gratitude to the Canaanites*, for hospitality received? Ah - they evidently do not have the military might of Egypt, to defend themselves. They are set upon, and done to as near extinction as the invaders can achieve!

The truth is that Abraham turned friends into enemies by his plan to take their lands. Canaan was made up of small nation states, even city states, whose populations seemed to be living peacefully alongside each other when he came calling. The one or two skirmishes we read of in Genesis were as *nothing*, compared to the unrelenting and merciless attacks that the newcomers were eventually to unleash upon their unsuspecting hosts, who had allowed the visitors to settle amongst them with no argument.

Yet, the Canaanites could have been forgiven for thinking that the newcomers posed a threat - for there were more than just a few of them. Besides his immediate family, we read of more than three hundred and eighteen trained, fighting men, born in his household (Gen 14), people whom we can assume were a whole retinue of servants (slaves), who would fight or herd the flocks of sheep and goats, as required. Female slaves were obviously busy having children, and taking care of all the household duties. Sara's maid, an Egyptian slave, Hagar, was given the duty of becoming a surrogate mother, when her mistress thought she could not bear children. It should have been cause for alarm amongst the Canaanites that these nomads, which, doubtless they *hoped* they were, came with a sizeable army. They would have been wise to be suspicious of the incomers, instead of selling them a field with a cave, for the burial of Sara. This gave them a claim on the land, and, if the three hundred and eighteen soldier/shepherds were as prolific as their master soon became, pressure on the land would shortly become acute.

Abraham's descendants, through his concubines Hagar and Keturah, and perhaps more, were left to integrate, or, at least, to live alongside the Canaanite tribes - for only seventy male descendants, through his son, Isaac - along with, presumably a similar number of uncounted females - are recorded as going off to Egypt, three generations later. Doubtless these Israelites (as they are called in the Bible), upon their return, kill off many of Abraham's *own* descendants, along with the hundreds of thousands of others they slaughter in Canaan.

What did Abrahm have, that has caused so much havoc in the world, from the terrorising and genocide of the Canaanites, a thousand years Before Christ, to the despair and upset of the inhabitants of that territory in modern times? It is his claim of a covenant with God, the belief that the land of others was a gift to Isaac's line from God, that has caused turmoil in the Middle East every thousand years since he lived.

What did Abraham have? He had arrogance, bluff, a dream, ambition, and determination. Did he have a covenant with God? It is a preposterous idea! There *can* be no such thing. And with *such* a man! He was a two-faced double-dealer, and, not knowing the truth from a lie, became his own first victim. Deceiving himself, he went on to make casualties of millions of others! *He* is the cause of most of the suffering recounted in the Old Testament, and also the cause of the suffering of the Palestinians nowadays.

The claim of a covenant with God has *got* to be self-delusion. Unfortunately, the Christian Church has perpetuated the error, teaching a covenant between God and Abraham, as part of Christianity. It cannot be! The partisan God, whom Abraham proclaims, is *unrecognisable* compared to the all-embracing

God of Jesus. A loving God *would not do* what the Old Testament claims God did. If God is not for everyone, he is *not* God. Our consciences and our common sense testify to that - and if religion violates our conscience, it is not true religion.

Abraham was accorded his fine reputation in Christianity as a mighty man of faith, when the first Christians, who had been brought up as Jews, took their Old Testament religion into their new faith, which saw Jesus as the Messiah, the fulfilment of the promise of a Saviour. They were not able to distinguish the two kinds of religion of the Old Testament - the one of land, law and killing - the other of justice, mercy and peace. They took the mixture, nay, the *confusion*, lock, stock and barrel, and incorporated the hotch-potch right into the middle of Christianity. Thus, we find Abraham and his ilk held up in the New Testament as paragons of virtue, shining examples of men of faith. The Church has gullibly believed the teaching handed down. Our theologians, instead of working out the significance of Jesus and his disciples being *persecuted* by the religion of the Old Testament, have continued down the ages with the old confusion, and regurgitated the old food.

The truth is that this "man of faith"displayed *no* faith, except in his own greed for lands that he saw and liked. Unlike a land God *could* have given him, an *empty* land, in which his people would have to do all the work, he fancied a land where the work had already been done by others, and so he chose Canaan, a land already planted with fields of grain, olives and vines, with cities and villages already built, which his descendants would usurp. That he was a man of faith, alotted this land by God, is *the biggest con in history*!

His faith was his determination to get this land for *some* of his own - notice only his favoured ones. A strange father, Abraham! Apart from that, there is ample demonstration of total *lack* of faith on his part. On the matter of children, he did not wait patiently on God. He eagerly enough, presumably, took Sara's maid as his concubine, to have children by, fathering Ishmael. But, instead of taking responsibility for the concubine he had taken, and the son he had fathered by her, when the going got tough - after Sara had her own child, Isaac, and no longer needed her slave's son - Abraham capitulated to her jealousy, and banished the no-longer-convenient pair of surrogates. This is inexcusable! This was not faith. Faith would have worked out a better way of dealing with the jealousy problem than what he did, for he sent the two off into the desert, to perish with heat, hunger and thirst, for all he seemed to care! The lies he told are more evidence of lack of faith in God to look after him. *If* he had had faith in God to look after him, he would have told the truth, trusting in God, instead of trusting in lies.

Thus the Old Covenant is built on the shaky foundation of this very flawed man, Abraham. He left his home, with his family and slaves, who were also an army, dreaming of a land of his own, and many descendants. He set about bringing his dreams to fruition in a very clever way - by saying it was *God*. That explanation impressed his own people. It was very convenient for them to have such an explanation for seizing a land, and murdering its inhabitants. But Abraham's view of things should *not* be meekly accepted by the Church. Delusion needs to be recognised. He should be judged by what he *did,* as well as be what he said. In that way, he has to be seen as a man whose covetous dream has caused untold suffering in the world.

The Dream of a Land
(In the style of a Scottish Ballad)

1   Abraham strolled through Canaan Land
      Woe, O woe to Canaan!
   With a mighty, three-hundred-strong fighting band.
      Weep and wail for Canaan!

2   For he came, and he eyed the milk and the honey,
      Woe, O woe to Canaan!
   And he bought him a field, with a show of money.
      But he dreamed to have *all* of Canaan.

3   He planted the dream in Isaac's head.
      Woe, O woe to Canaan!
   "The Lord will give *us* this Land", he said.
      Weep and wail for Canaan!

4   Isaac planted the dream in Jacob's head.
      Woe, O woe to Canaan!
   "This land is going to be *ours*", he said.
      Weep and wail for Canaan!

5   Jacob planted the dream in his twelve sons' heads.
         Woe, O woe to Canaan!
     And they murdered the Hivites in their beds.
         That's how they treated Canaan!

6   But Joseph escaped their murderous hands,
     When they sold him to Egypt in slavery.
     They followed, taking the dream with them -
     The dream that inspired their knavery.

7   They nurtured the dream for four hundred years.
         Woe, O woe to Canaan
     In Egypt they rally, in the desert they muster,
         For the ravage of innocent Canaan.

8   Where is the milk? *Blood* flows now in the streets,
         In the city streets of Canaan!
     In the Land of Honey, the blood of the sweet,
         When the killers came to Canaan!

9   None left alive in Jericho,
         Ai, Makkedah, Libnah, Eglon;
     None left alive in Lachish, Debir,
         Hazor nor Hebron.

10   Weep for the kings of Canaan Land,
         For their exhibition death;
     Trampled, their necks - pierced, hung on trees -
         Canaan's dying breath!

11   They plunder and steal, drink the milk, eat their fill
         Of the fat of the Land of Canaan,
     Building up strength - the strength needed to kill
         The rest of the darlings of Canaan.

CHAPTER 5

MOSES

"Now kill all the boys. And kill every woman who has been with a man, but save for yourselves all the female virgins." (Numbers 31 v 17-18)

The above quotation from the Old Testament was not the Pharaoh of Egypt speaking - the Pharaoh was not so depraved. No, this was Moses speaking, whom the Christian Church, blind to his depravity, hails as a man of God! The killing of the Canaanites, instituted by Moses, although accredited to God, are crimes against humanity, which the Church, far from condemning, has traditionally praised, and called "desirable". Some eminent Christian scholars, "Doctors of Divinity", have even gone into print, calling the genocide of the Canaanites "a moral necessity"! I hope the Church will come to see the error of its ways, and publicly repudiate such morally untenable judgments.

Christian children learn early to love Moses, in the story of the Baby in the Bullrushes. They rejoice that Baby Moses is saved, and rightly lament the slaughter of innocent Hebrew baby boys, by the order of the wicked Pharaoh - for plainly, *anyone* who orders the murder of babies is wicked.

By the same standard, then, we have to call the grown-up Moses wicked - for *he* ordered the murder of countless *more* babies, as well as of older children and adults. What is more, most of those whose deaths he ordered had never seen him, or spoken to him, or harmed him, or his people, in any way. In fact, their ancestors had treated *his* ancestors very well. Without any reason, except that he wanted their land for his people, he set about the annihilation of the people of Canaan.

Even *before* the Burning Bush vision, Moses had blood on his hands. After killing an Egyptian, he fled the country to escape justice (Exodus 2 v 15). Here is *another* "man of faith" displaying no faith at all in God to see him through the term of punishment he might receive. And, if he feared the death penalty (which, we discover later, is his own *favourite* punishment), he was not planning on trusting in *God* to save him! Yet, in Midian, the faithless fugitive finds religion in a big way, and he believes he encounters God at The Burning Bush (Ex 3).

Who *is* this God? Moses asks this very question. Obviously he is not the God of *all* people, the God of Creation, who must love all people equally - for the God who answers here, giving the enigmatic reply, "I am who I am", also goes on to say that he is the God of Abraham, Isaac and Jacob (the Hebrew patriarchs), the God who made a covenant with them, to give them a land, in exchange for obedience to his commands. This is the God of *one line of one people*. This is the God of the dream of a land, and of killing for it, the God of Israel, a *territorial* God - yet, Christianity teaches this fiercely nationalistic God as the God of all!

This *confusion* of a God - who is conveniently *supposed* to be the God of all, who is conveniently portrayed as *moral*, even *holy*, yet inspires his followers to mass slaughter, as well as all kinds of cruelty, oppression and lasciviousness - this is the *confusion* of a God that Christianity proclaims! Moses' encounter with his God at the Burning Bush is taken to be *everyone's* God in Christianity, even though he says he is *not*! In Church and Sunday School, Moses' *murdering* is glossed over, and no inconsistency is noticed between his supposed faith in God, and his fleeing from justice, nor - which is even *more* inconsistent - the fugitive from justice goes on to become the *champion of law and order*! Indeed, in one children's address I heard in church, the minister contended that, since Moses had killed a man, he *had* to flee the country - as though no one, at least no Jew or Christian, should even *think* of answering for their crimes! This is the kind of ludicrous conclusion one arrives at from the spurious logic that operates when one accepts liars and murderers as men of God.

Of course, he *might* have repented of his crime. But if he *had* repented, he would have gone back to Egypt, to face the judicial system, in the faith that God would look after him. After all, the books of Genesis, Exodus, Leviticus, Numbers, and Deuteronomy, attributed to his authorship, make the claim that God softens and hardens hearts at will, especially the Pharaoh's! So, God could have softened Pharaoh's heart, to let him get away with murder. But no - he chose the other way to get away with murder - and Moses *always* got away with murder - he fled the country, and stayed away forty years! In fact, there is no record anywhere that Moses ever repented of *any* of the thousands of deaths he caused, even of his own people - on the contrary, he attributed them to *God*!

Man of God or master magician? Certainly, Moses can mesmerise an audience, and does so all his life. Pharaoh's magicians do not compare with him in the competitions that they have - but then, *he* is credited with writing the Bible account of them... However, his stroke of genius is that he does not claim superiority for himself, but says it is *God*. Doubtless he believes it. From the stick that becomes a snake, in Ex 4, to the killing of fifteen thousand of his own people, who rejected him as leader, in Numbers 16, *God* gets all the credit. On top of all this, after tyrannising and terrorising the people for forty years in the desert wanderings, the verdict given by those whom he ruled with a rod of iron is, "Moses was a meek man"! Well, he *wrote* it for them, at least...

The cleverest aspect of giving all the credit (or blame) to God for the countless deaths, was that people were afraid, not just of the man, but of his God. If God was on Moses' side, to rebel against him was to rebel against God. Moses let the people know that, in no uncertain terms. Soon, no one dared to raise a voice against him. This is understandable of the people who had to live their daily lives under his command. It is *not* so understandable for the Christian Church to champion this man: he is the original terrorist of the Bible, and a trainer of terrorists *par excellence*.

To their credit, the Israelites, upon leaving Egypt, do *not* want to terrorise others. They appear to be perfectly nice, normal people, without any grudge against their neighbours, and certainly have no intention of killing anyone. They find themselves suddenly uprooted from their everyday lives and daily routine, to a life of camping in the desert, with nothing much to do all day, except collect their daily ration of manna to eat, *and obey the dictates of Moses*. And his dictates grow and grow! First of all there are The Ten Commandments, but soon the ten are expanded into more than six hundred - and very strict they are, with many innocent little activities, called "work" made sins, if they are done on the Sabbath. Not only so, but many of those piffling little sins carry the death penalty! The shock of the sudden uprooting turns to trauma, as their leader implements his new law, claiming it is God's Law. More than ever, to disobey Moses comes to be seen as disobeying God - thus he can justify *anything* he does, and even justify the death penalty for next to nothing!

I should think it is not easy to turn fairly timid people into killing machines - especially to get them to kill people who have never done them any harm, and, more especially, to kill babies - but Moses achieved this feat. He even achieved it in the face of having delivered them a *Commandment from God*, which said "Thou shalt *not* kill"! But then, the whole religion of a Covenant and a Promised Land is based on breaking every one of The Ten Commandments. So much for the Law, famously written on tablets of stone - Moses spent his life breaking every vestige of morality in them! How did he succeed in turning normal people, who must, by nature, be disinclined to kill others, into the monsters they became, who were prepared to kill everyone inhabiting the land they wanted?

First of all, he established himself as a man of God; not just *any* man of God, but a man who had *seen* God, and who *"spoke to God face to face, just as a man speaks to his friend"* (Ex 33 v 11). That is some reputation to enjoy! It is exactly the reputation which enabled him to tyrannise the nation with its consent!

Secondly, he quelled any opposition. In the early days, many of the Israelites complained that they did not want to go to the "Promised Land". They talked about returning to Egypt. Life was not so bad there; at least, they always had plenty to eat - lovely fish, fruit and vegetables (Numbers 11 v 5). Nor did most of the spies sent out have any stomach for the evident struggle it would be to wrest the land from its owners. They came back from their sorties with samples of wonderful crops, but reported that , "the people are huge, and the cities are fortified", recommending that they should *not* try to take them (Num 13). Moses would have none of it, and *no one* was allowed to contradict him: his word was God's word, he claimed. The ten who disagreed with Moses were killed - of course !

Yet, some brave dissenters tried to elect another leader (Num 14 v 4) and return to Egypt. It is no surprise to read that they were not long for this world. Opposition to Moses spelled *death* for the opponent. The shock is that as many as fifteen thousand were put to death, for daring to side with the rivals. Their deaths, of course, "pour encourager les autres", were all credited to God - and still are, by the Church! To oppose Moses was to oppose God - and the Church agrees. This pattern had been set earlier, when the Levites had been encouraged to kill three thousand of their fellow - Israelites (Exodus 32 v 28).

Moses knew his campaign of terror was working, when the people brought to him a man accused of collecting firewood on the Sabbath. Punishment for this "offence" had already been specified as death, yet the people hesitated, obviously reluctant to carry out this harsh punishment, for such a trivial crime. They are reported to be "not clear what should be done to him" (Num 15 v 34). This was Moses' big chance to find out how far he could get them to go, and he seized it with both hands. "He must be put to death", he told them. The whole community was made to stone the poor man to death. Moses knew that the first murder is the hardest to commit. He was finding it easy, himself, by then. Now they *all* had blood on their hands. Things were going his way. In fact, he knew then he had them in the palm of *his* hands!

Thirdly, he identified religion, not with morality, but with *blood*. The Ten Commandments became the smoke-screen of a religion based on morality, for a religion that was primarily concerned with blood sacrifices. *Blood* became the symbol for *God*. He instituted covenant rituals, where the congregation was bespattered with blood. Thus, the people came to associate *killing* and *blood* with *God*. This was a very useful association, for it meant that the population were convinced they were doing God's will when they rampaged through Canaan, becoming drenched in more blood than any of them, even in their worst nightmares, could ever have dreamt of spilling.

The very blades used for all the slaughter started with a religious use. Knives, of course, were needed in the preparation of food. From the time of the Passover Meal, just before leaving Egypt, food became a *huge* part of the national religion. After the Tabernacle was built, it even became illegal to slaughter in the field an animal they intended to eat: it *had* to be done, ritually, by the priests in the Tabernacle, and later, of course, in the Temple. The punishment for breaking this new law was death - of course!

Knives and cutting tools galore must have been needed for all the work involved in building and fitting out the Tabernacle in the Wilderness, this House of the Lord, the precursor to the Temple. A special box, the Ark of the Covenant, had to be beautifully carved, before being overlaid with gold. The giant tent, which was to house the Covenant Box, required much delicate work on all its elaborate furnishings and fittings, with many blades necessary for the fine work. Here is a nation busy using blades for the glory of God. The book of Exodus gives many details - of the dimensions of the structure, of poles, rings, curtains and clothes needed for the sacrificial rituals, involving the slaughter of animals on a huge scale, which became the main focus of their whole lives. Blades were not lacking - and all the work they were used for, was part of the *worship* in the desert.

Yet *more* flint blades were required at the end of the journey, as we read in Joshua 5 v 2. These were for circumcising all the males born in the forty years since leaving Egypt. Thus, when the nation emerged from the desert, murderous blades were not lacking, for the mass slaughter they would become engaged in. All the fear of their religious masters, and the association of blood, killing, and blind obedience, with religion and with God, gave them the psychological blindness, and impetus needed, to become the most ruthless invaders the Canaanites had ever heard of, or could ever conceive of. Their atrocities soon became legendary.

The "wilderness years", used in sermons by Christian ministers to describe a nation becoming more and more *godly*, as it approached its "Promised Land", were, in fact, the very *opposite*. They were years when the nation was trained in blind obedience to their leader through fear, and when they were trained how to kill, and feel no pity, remorse or guilt!

Threats, curses, excessive punishments, constant fear, forced complicity in murder - no wonder the nation was traumatised! And all the while, Moses pretended only to want the best for his people, nothing more. By the end of the process they did not feel he was forcing them to do anything against their will! He dangled the carrot of all the marvellous things they would come in for, if only they obeyed him (and, therefore, the Lord). At first they were not told they would need to murder the inhabitants of the land - they would only need to walk into it, he said, for the Lord would make the nations flee in terror, leaving everything for them to enjoy (Ex 23 v 27). But that story changed along the way, and the grim news, in the end, was that the people were going to have to fight for the prizes, after all, because the disobliging Canaanites did not plan to make themselves homeless and starving, *even to oblige the Lord*! But the prizes would be worth fighting for - cities ready built, houses full of things they did not put in them, wells ready dug, water in abundance, mature vineyards and olive groves... as listed in Deut 6 v 10-11. Yes, they were going to have to fight, but, they could be assured, the Lord would be with them, and give them victory. It was *the Lord's* fight!

There is no greater incentive to people than to believe God is on their side. They *dare* not give up, for if they do, they are letting *God* down, and thereby might suffer eternal loss! The motivation to keep going when, otherwise, they might have stopped, is immense. They are prepared to be as brutal as can be, believing they represent good fighting evil. They also feel no compassion for their victims, and no guilt. *This* was the terrible psychological state that the Israelites ended up in, at the hands of Moses. He took nice, normal people, certainly with a strange, religious dream - but we all have our dreams - and turned them into one of the most fearsome fighting forces in history. By first terrorising them, he turned them into terrorists.

This story is written in the first five books of the Christian Bible - but this is not the way the Church teaches it! How *it* teaches it, I will deal with in Chapter 8.

CHAPTER 6

THE CANAANITES

"Que m'avaient-ils fait? Nulle offense!"

In La Fontaine's brilliant poem, *Les animaux malades de la peste*, the lion calls a conference of all the animals, to find out who has angered the gods, and caused the plague to be inflicted on them. The guilty one will be sacrificed to appease the divine wrath, even if it has to be himself. He is willing to confess that, as well as eating many sheep, who had never done him any harm, he has sometimes, also, eaten the shepherd - but he thinks that everyone should confess, just as he has done, to see who the worst sinner is. The carnivores soon conclude that they do the world a *favour* if they eat people - that to devour members of that detestable, human species is to rid the world of *trash*! Come the turn of the donkey, he shamefacedly confesses that, once, he ate some grass in the monastery meadow, which he had no right to do... The screams and shrieks of righteous indignation from all present, were testimony enough that *this* was the cause of all their woe. The donkey was sacrificed.

La Fontaine was criticising the French judicial system of his day, which, he claimed, did not accord justice to the humble and weak. The Christian Church, however, has never *yet* criticised the similar justice system of its holy book, the Bible, where the strong and powerful kill off the weak - or rather, the ruthless and unscrupulous massacre, with impunity, the people of good manners and good morals. On the contrary, the Christian Church continues, in the face of all the barbarity and arrogance recorded there, to *condone* the sacrifice of the humble and innocent Canaanite people, upon the the say-so of the murderers. Just because the murderers said it was God who told them to commit the murders, the gullible Church has blindly believed, and taught this vicious doctrine, all over the world, for two thousand years!

Could it begin now to see that it is *impossible* for a loving God to command this, that such a portrayal of God is *blasphemous* and a *travesty*? I hope so. If the Church continues to fail to condemn the mass-murder of the Canaanites, it is consenting to genocide. This consent is not by default It is actively assented to in sermons and written commentaries which praise the nation and its leaders who effected the slaughter. Certainly, it is becoming a bit more embarrassing for them to say, "the Canaanites deserved to die because they worshipped idols", but they used to preach this quite readily, and, doubtless, some still do, in Fundamentalist circles. In fact, we all know that idol-worship is *not* a sin, nor a crime, yet the Church has traditionally taught that, three thousand years ago, in Canaan, *it was worse than genocide,* and that to murder an idol-worshipper was a righteous act! The logic of this teaching is that "murder is good, and genocide is better, so long as you claim that God told you to do it"! Anyone should be able to see that this is *outrageous*, yet, still in many Christian circles, the thinking persists that, "If the Bible says it's so, it must be so".

One more point must be made here, which is that devious people accuse others of their own crimes. This is also what the Hebrews did in relation to the Canaanites - accused them of their own sexual sins, as their own scriptures testify. This, in fact, compounds the *crimes against humanity* called *virtue* in the Bible: the Israelites accused others of being guilty of their own sins, and then used the accusation as an excuse to eliminate them! Of course, it was only a ploy to justify seizing their lands.

The Church has failed to see that the vengeful, territorial God of Israel is *not* the loving God of all people, and it tries to say that he is. But how can the God who inspired hate, war and genocide be the God of Jesus? He cannot. The God of the Old Testament was invented by Abraham to gratify his territorial ambitions. This version of God was passed, seemingly innocuously, down generations of Israelites, until, under Moses, the theory began, dramatically and drastically, to be implemented. Woe to anyone who did not agree with Moses - Israelite *or* Canaanite! Not to kowtow to him meant death for the Israelite: just to live in or near Canaan meant death to the Canaanite.

"We came unto the land whither thou sentest us, and surely it floweth with milk and honey, and this is the fruit of it. Nevertheless, the people be strong that live in that land, and the cities are walled, and very great; and moreover, we saw the children of Anak there. The Amalekites dwell in the land to the south; and the Hittites and the Jebusites, and the Amorites, dwell in the mountains; and the Canaanites dwell by the sea, and by the coast of Jordan." And Caleb stilled the people before Moses, and said, "Let us go up at once, and possess it, for we are well able to overcome it." (Num 13)

The fruit referred to was an *enormous* cluster of grapes, which the spies carried back on a pole, to show the Israelites the fertility, and therefore the desirability, of the land. The Anakites were very big people, whom the Old Testament even claims were giants, descended from the Nephilim, "sons of God", who came down from the sky, and had carnal relations with beautiful women on Earth, and produced this race (Gen 6)! One could have thought that such a pedigree might have inspired some respect in Moses (who spoke to God, as with a friend), but no - *land* was at stake, and no descendants of God or gods were going to stop Moses, Caleb and the rest from acquiring it.

The word "Canaanite" is usually used to refer to all of the indigenous tribes of the land besieged by the Israelites in the Old Testament, although, as the above text shows, the Canaanites were only one of many tribes. The Canaanite tribe's territory seems to have been in two parts, and widely spread. Perhaps they were the most numerous of the tribes. Ever aware of the possibility of attack, cities were walled, but the population obviously worked the surrounding land during the day, to produce their food. The whole region seems to have been peaceful and productive when "the holy nation" arrived at its borders. The peace was shattered for the next three hundred years, and the crops became the invaders' food (Joshua 5 v 12), which was one of the reasons they wanted the native population dead.

Perhaps the only holy names in the Old Testament are those of the people sacrificed to the covetous lust of the priestly nation. It was Moses' intention to exterminate them, like the vermin he thought they were, and, along with them, their *names* (Deut 7 v 24). Ironically, it was his determination to do this by means of *religion*, that has kept the names very much alive - for they came into Christianity, via the scriptures of Judaism, as part of Christian holy writ, and Christian missionaries disseminated the names all over the world! By writing down the names they wished to destroy, the Old Testament writers inadvertantly preserved them.

"Canaanite" comprises such names as Amalekite, Amorite, Arkite, Arvadite, Avim, Anakim, Bashanite, Emmim, Gebalite, Girgashite, Hamathite, Hittite, Hivite, Horim, Ishmaelite, Jebusite, Kadmonite, Kenite, Kenizzite, Perizzite, Rephaim, Sinite, Zamzummin, Zemarite, Zuzim. There are other names, such as Adullamite. This would be someone from the city of Adullam, which was Jebusite. Along with these wonderful names, there are the Philistines, usually named separately from the Canaanites, since they were a target for later attack - their territory being farther west than the first round of targets - and the Phoenicians, usually referred to by the names of their main cities, Tyre and Sidon. These were thriving ports long before Abraham appeared on the scene, around 1800 BC. Ammonites and Moabites were also classed along with Canaanites, although the Bible claims they were descended from Lot, Abraham's nephew. This kinship, like Ishmael's, did not save them from the ravages of the Israelites.

There is a list, in Joshua 12, of thirty-one kings killed, named by their capital cities: the Kings of Jericho, Ai, Jerusalem, Hebron, Jarmuth, Lachish, Eglon, Gezer, Debir, Geder, Hormah, Arad, Libnah, Adullam, Makkedah, Bethel, Tapuah, Hepher, Aphek, Lasharon, Madon, Hazor, Shimron Meron, Acshaph, Taanach, Megiddo, Kedesh, Jokneam, Dor, Goyim, Tizrah. The list is not exhaustive, for it does not mention those killed east of the Jordan River, King Sihon of Heshbon, King Og of Bashaan, Baalam, Balak, nor the five kings of Midian - Evi, Rekem, Zur, Hur and Reba. How many more? Yet, these are an indication of countless thousands of people slain - it could even be millions.

The Edomites' land was expressly forbidden by Moses to be taken (Deut 2 v 5), for they were reckoned to be descendants of Jacob's twin brother Esau. (*They* had already taken that land from the Horim.) Yet, the Edomites were constantly plagued, later, by the Israelites - so much for the Lord's command!

The writers, in recording their theology and their history, convinced of their superiority over every other nation and religion, presumably did not realize that they were also recording their arrogance, racism, greed and ruthlessness. That is natural enough; we are *all* blinded by self-love, if we are not very careful. What is amazing is the lack of criticism by Christians, whatever nation they belong to, of the barbarity recorded for all to read, albeit by default. Such is the power of our upbringing to stunt our perceptiveness

The winners wrote the history. That does not mean that the winners were right. What it *does* mean is that the history will have their bias. Their bias may say that they won because God made them win, but we do not have to believe it. In reality they may have won because they were more cunning and ruthless.

Certainly, the motivation of the Israelites to take the Canaanites' land was phenomenal. What nation could be expected to guess the psychology that made them ready to raid, kill, plunder and lay waste, with a determination unlike anything they had ever seen before? Those who wage war believing God is on their side, even when it is obvious to any right-minded person that this could not *possibly* be so, are the assailants most to be feared. They are capable of *any* atrocity when "God is on their side"! The Assyrians and Babylonians, for *all* their idols, were much more merciful to the Israelites, when they conquered them, than ever their prisoners had been. They resettled them - see 2 Kings 17 v 6, where the writer testified that they were alive at the time of writing - thereby, inadvertantly, showing the despised idol-worshippers to be immeasurably more humane than the people who claimed to be godly.

The Israelites took no prisoners. The book of Joshua makes grim reading. That Christian professors in Faculties of Divinity, who ought to have some ability to think, can have taught for so long this bloodthirsty story as God's will is astonishing. Their blind acquiescence to this evil perpetrated in God's name, for their students then to disseminate in churches, and worse, for their missionaries to teach all over the world, surely cannot continue any longer. Our conscience tells us it is wickedness of the first order, for a nation to besiege city after city, full of people who had never in their lives done one iota of harm to the attackers, or had even *seen* an Israelite before, and to leave none of the inhabitants alive. How is it that our theologians did not discern this?

The answer could be that they have no real spiritual or moral discernment. Traditional Christianity has been led by "blind guides", like those in the scriptures they taught, unthinkingly reiterating ancient biassed history and theology. Thinking themselves wise, they became the biggest fools. But their foolishness is not comedy; it is *tragedy*, for it has led to the repetition, over the last fifty years, of what happened three thousand years ago to the Canaanites - the taking of a land from its rightful inhabitants, the Palestinians. *Judaism* can have Moses and Joshua as heroes, Christianity *cannot*, for they were leaders waging a merciless war of attrition against peaceful people, who could otherwise have lived out their lives happily, farming to feed their families, had not a genocidal army come calling, putting every man, woman and child to the sword. It was *never* God who masterminded such wickedness, and it can never be right for Christianity to say that it was.

No wonder most of the Arabs today claim to be descendants of Abraham. Quite likely they are, since the genes of the Canaanites were largely destroyed! Only on the fringes of the land, as we are told in Joshua 11 v 22, in tones of regret, did a few escape the murderous blades: "No Anakites were left in Israelite territory; but there were some survivors in Gaza, Gath and Ashdod". They became targets another day!

The sole group of Canaanites to survive in the land, was one part of the Hittite tribe from Gibeon. They survived only because they acted out a desperate ruse on the invaders, whose rapacity had become known. These terrorised and terrified people yet had the presence of mind to work out the only *possible* way to be *allowed,* by the people playing God, to live. This was by making themselves look unkempt, as if they were on the road, and saying they had no land there, that they were just passing through. They offered to be slaves to the Israelites in perpetuity, if only they could be allowed their lives. The masters agreed, and even at that, some grumbled, and wished they had not made the promise, so that they could wipe them all out, as they did the other tribes (Joshua 9 v 9). We might guess that many were, indeed, later killed - by King Saul. No pity for the Canaanites, no remorse for their removal from the face of the Earth is ever uttered in the Bible, nor yet, officially, by the Christian Church - as *must happen* if the Church wishes to remain morally credible and respectable.

Instead of feeling that something must be far wrong with their religion, when it involved so much killing, the reverse was true, for the Israelites of the Old Testament. Their euphoria was such that they credited God with physically helping them, by showering down hailstones on the fleeing victims of their atrocities (Joshua 10 v 11-14)! They even claimed God made the sun stop rising and setting for a day, in celebration of their massacres! If this is not proof of an overblown imagination, what is? Yet, *some* Christian preachers have accepted those verses as proof that God *was* on the side of the Israelites, even if they give other explanations, such as eclipses, or bad weather, for what Michael Prior calls in his book, THE BIBLE AND COLONIALISM, "divinely approved, divinely mandated outrages".

The attackers continually call their warring "revenge". This, too, is a *lie*, for "revenge" means "inflicting hurt *in return for a harm done*". But the Canaanites had never done them any harm. They had never *seen* their attackers before. Their ancestors, of five hundred years previous, had treated Abraham's people very well indeed. He, and the hundreds with him, had shared the land peacefully, until some of them chose to go off to Egypt for a better life, during a famine. Revenge was not possible, for no harm had been done; *thanks* were due!

St Paul, in Acts 13 v 19, makes matter-of-fact mention, with no intended criticism, of the killing of seven Canaanite nations by his ancestors in the process of settling the land. He was a Jew, and, perhaps, could not be expected to reinterpret their history for them, or even, for the Church. After all, *non-*

Jewish Christians have also failed to condemn the slaughter. Paul already had his hands full, reinterpreting his old religion with Jesus as the Messiah, the Anointed One, the long-awaited Leader and Saviour. Circumcision was not to be inflicted on non-Jewish Christians, and the Jewish dietary laws were to become obsolete for Jewish Christians. But those decisions were not straightforward, and were much argued over in the Early Church (Acts 15).

Even if St Paul, and Jesus too, failed to condemn the slaughter of the Canaanites, it is high time for the Church to do so. The people whom Jesus befriended and championned, over against the Scribes, Pharisees and Sadduccees - the religious sections of the society - were, quite possibly, the descendants of the Canaanites - those few, *tragically* few, who survived. It was the underclass, called Sinners, who barely saw themselves as Jews, who loved the new message of God on the side of the despised and the oppressed. Perhaps they were despised because they were only half-Jewish, originally - offspring of the illicit liaisons with the poor, Canaanite girls, doled out to the Jewish men, part of "the spoils of war" and therefore, not to be accepted as belonging to "The Lord's People".

It was this despised section of the community that was happy to hear the good news that God loved them (Matthew 5). The religious Jews *could* have been attracted to this message, too, and become disciples - and, indeed, some were, and did, like Nicodemus (John 3) and Joseph of Arimathea (Luke 23 v 51). However, in the main, the powerful, religious leaders were highly offended by this new teaching and preaching, and determined to have it stopped, even if that meant trumping up a charge. A lesser penalty than the death penalty they were not willing to accept, either. They saw that Jesus was as much for the non-Jew as for the Jew, and they would not tolerate it. The Early Church was always in "fear of the Jews", ie the religious section of the community (see Acts of the Apostles).

Nowhere does Jesus' teaching condone the killing of the Canaanites. Rather, his teaching is, "Those whom you deemed were unloved by God are *not* unloved: God loves them". No wonder Judaism rejected him! It is time that Christianity rejected the religion that rejected Jesus. Unrepentant murderers have *nothing* to teach anyone about morality or God, and the Church needs to recognise this fact. The Church's failure to call evil *"evil"* has already caused untold suffering in the world throughout the past two thousand years. By keeping the Old Testament war ethic, the medieval Church was able to justify calling the Crusades. This ethic also enabled so-called Christians to sail around the world, with guns and cannons, threatening defenceless people, taking their lands and their goods, often, also, their lives, inflicting untold suffering and loss upon whoever they wished. They were able to justify their atrocites from their holy book, which justified similar deeds. The evil goings-on in this book, accepted in Christianity as God's will, are what led the western Allies, after the Second World War, to give away the Land of Palestine to foreigners (ie people born outside Palestine), because their ancestors had lived in it for a spell, after massacring the inhabitants three thousand years ago.

Christianity brought about the climate for the setting-up of the State of Israel in another nation's country, making it possible for history to be repeating itself, at the present time, on the same soil. Many Palestinians have been killed only for defending their land just, as the Canaanites were. The incomers again got away with mass slaughter, which one *might* have thought was not so easy, in modern times. Has any Israeli ever been brought to book for the massacres at Al Dawayima, Al Husayniyya, Al Tira, Al Qastal, Ayn al Zaytun, Ayn Ghazal, Balad al Shaykh, Dayr Yasin, Jaba, Jish, Khubbayza, Qalunya, Safsaf, Saliha, Sa'sa', Saris, or for any of the other massacres of 1947-8? Was anyone brought to book for the murder of the UN Mediator, Count Folke Bernadotte? How many have ever been brought to court, even, for the murder of countless Palestinians? Very few! However, nowadays, more subtle and surreptitious ways of appropriating the land are usually employed.

Because Christianity failed to condemn the slaughter of the Canaanites and the occupation of Canaan in the Bible, it paved the way for a similar thing to happen to the Palestinians in Palestine.

CHAPTER 7

JERICHO

Jericho, a very ancient city, was walled, to protect its inhabitants, who farmed this fertile, low-lying oasis by the Dead Sea. The smug, even gloating, Chapter 6 of Joshua *should* be told, in the Church, as the *heart-breaking* story of its siege. Moses had primed the nation, and set the attack on Canaan in motion, approving, also, of the massacring of nations on the east of the Jordan, which were not even part of the "promise" (Num 21). Joshua was Moses' successor. As usual, the killing was made out to be a religious duty, and religious fervour was high, following mass circumcision of the males, and the Passover Feast, in the weeks and days before the attack.

"The city and everything in it must be totally destroyed, as an offering to the Lord." v 17

   - "An *offering to the Lord*"? What kind of God would want such and offering?

"Only the prostitute, Rahab, and her family, will be spared, for she hid our spies." v 17

   - They were engaged in *the Lord's work* in the brothel, were they?

"...Silver, gold and bronze or iron...is to be put into the Lord's treasury." v 19

   - This God is unhealthily interested in material things. Would it be wise to trust *such* a God, or the people who preach him?

"...With their swords they slew everyone in the city - men, women, young and old. They also killed all the cattle, sheep and donkeys." v 21

   - *Everyone*, down to the smallest baby - and every animal, down to the tiniest kitten - killed - as a *present* to the Lord? Some present! Some Lord! The killers are people claiming to be holy. Not only so - their religion is supposed to educate the *world* in morality and spirituality. Christianity says so, as well as Judaism!

"...They set fire to the city, and burned it to the ground, except..."(what they had looted for "the Lord's treasury"). v 24

- How can Christians down the ages have accepted this as all right? It is incredible! But this is taught as God's inscrutable will, which we have to accept. No thanks! It is manifestly contrary to the New Testament teaching of a God who loves everyone; but this deters the Church not a whit!

"Rahab and her family live in Israel to this day." v 25

- Did she, one wonders, live to hate the Israelites for what they did to her people; or to hate herself for betraying them? Could she ever grow to *like* her adopted nation; or herself?

"Cursed be anyone who rebuilds the city of Jericho." v 26

- This ultimate insult is added to ultimate injury. They did not even *want* the city, nor the animals! They wanted its fertile fields, with their abundant produce, its olive groves and vineyards, fruitful from being well-tended and worked. They had already started to eat the Canaanites' food without a "Thank you" (Josh 5 v 12). *This* was what the marauders had come for - a land all tilled, planted and bearing crops - a land "flowing with milk and honey". There, the dates hang from the palm trees, like huge bunches of sweets from God, and the water-melons bulge, offering to assuage the thirst of the parched desert traveller. This place, where Nature's goodness and generosity abound, as if apologising for the sparseness of the desert it inhabits, witnessed a "godliness", whose greed knew no bounds - and no apology for the massacre of all the inhabitants.

"So the Lord was with Joshua, and he became famous throughout the country." v 27

- He certainly became famous - but it was *not* because God was with him!

Bad enough to preach about this episode as "a great battle where the Lord gave his people victory over an abominable foe" to adults, Christian *children* are taught to rejoice at the terrorising of the hapless victims, before the final onslaught. Dramatic presentations are made of "the Lord's Army" marching daily, once round the city, and, on the last day, seven times, playing their trumpets. Do they ever think of playing the role of the terrified citizens, under siege for a week, starving, and probably dead from thirst, before the week is up, because the invaders are occupying their stores and springs? Do they teach the children, also, to plunge knives into little babies, if any are still alive at the end of the week's siege? If not, why not - if it was such a godly episode?

Stop such sacrilege! - Teach the children to sympathise with the innocent victims of an unholy rage, instead of despising them! Teach them that God does *not* inspire mass murder! *That* is inspired by hatred and greed, and *never* by God. "Joshua fought the Battle of Jericho", goes the song - but this is a lie, for there was *no* battle - there was siege and massacre, after a week, of already dying people. The murderers were not holy, but deluded people, determined to take everything they wanted by force. Weep for Jericho!

CHAPTER 8

"MORAL MENACE"

The traditional teaching in Christianity, on the slaughter of the Canaanites, has this summary in The Bible Reader's Encyclopaedia and Concordance, edited by the Rev. W.M. Clow, D.D. "That the inhabitants of the land were to be destroyed has been the subject of much criticism. It should be remembered that the judgment upon their sins was long deferred. To have preserved the people in the midst of Israel, would have involved a physical and moral menace that could not be justified." (Entry on The Book of Joshua)

The above quotation is the most *disgraceful* theology one can imagine, voicing the belief that *God* was using the Israelites of old, to punish a nation of idol-worshippers - *this* God being self-confessedly jealous of idols (Ex 20 v 5)! This theology means that *idol-worshippers= bad, murderers= good* (as long as the victims of the murderers are idol-worshippers. Dr. Clow had evidently not noticed, in his Bible studies, how the Israelites all had idols and images, if they could afford them, for worship in their homes (Judges 18 v 20).

It is a tragedy that the Church's very Doctors of Divinity have been so devoid of moral and spiritual discernment, that they could utter such wicked sentiments, and even write them in reference books. Unfortunately, the rubbish expressed in these is still part of Church doctrine - why else would Moses and Joshua be hailed as "men of God"? Yet not many ministers nowadays, at least of the Church of Scotland, would be as bold as Dr. Clow, and voice the teaching in such stark terms. Why not? Because they *know in their hearts* there is something far wrong with it - but, still, it stands, part of the baggage of keeping the Old Testament as holy writ, unrepudiated. Fortunately, Liberation Theology is now challenging the traditional teaching on the Bible.

The passage, quoted above, reveals the very lowest ability in moral judgment. No wonder the Church is in trouble, when it has doctrines (albeit usually unspoken) that say "murder is better than idol-worship", and Doctors of Divinity who cannot see that is wrong! Church members cannot stomach such moral filth. This is the poison that has contaminated Christianity, from the ridiculous claims of Abraham, the many murders and massacres of the seizing of Canaan, the Crusades of the Middle Ages, down to the havoc, distress and despair that has been caused to the Palestinian nation, and is *still* being caused by the erroneous doctrines that have been peddled for two thousand years. Such a judgment displays the moral and spiritual arrogance still prevalent in some branches of the Church, and they have got away with it for far too long. Their exasperating "holier than thou" pose, should be enough to warn us to beware - to take everything they say with a big pinch of salt, and to examine it in the light of our own individual consciences, which are, by the look of things, *much* more reliable than their collective conscience.

John Knox, in the sixteenth century, had a vision of Scotland where everyone would be educated in the reading and writing of Latin and Greek. The aim was that congregations would be able to check the validity, from Bible manuscripts, of what they were being taught in the churches, and, if necessary, correct the teachers. What is needed *now* is for congregations to do a *moral* check, using their consciences, to see whether the *Bible is saying what is right*! If what is written does not accord with conscience, then it is *wrong*. We must always be prepared to do our own thinking, and not blindly trust *even a book reported to be "holy"*. Who said it was holy? They could be wrong. What does it mean that a book is "holy"? It only means that it is *set apart for use in worship*. "Holy" does *not* mean "infallible". Judge by the sentiments in the Bible!

And people *are* thinking for themselves. In fact, they are away ahead of theologians, ministers and priests, who are often hidebound in their thinking. People in Scotland have some education, and some confidence in their own judgments. They have listened to too many sermons that do not make sense, noticed too many *revolting* verses in the Bible, like Psalm 137 v 9, and read too many sickening statements, like the one at the beginning of this chapter - and they have left the Church by the thousand! Who can blame them? The Church tries to work out reasons for its dwindling membership, and lights on this or that, in which there may be some truth. But it is not good enough to be putting it down to other attractions on Sundays, or to the frivolous attitude of people, either non-members, or members who stop attending services. I speak constantly to people who tell me they are greatly troubled by by the teaching of the Church, and particularly the Old Testament killings. They know there is something wrong, and they want it put right. The ordinary Church member in Scotland is ready to challenge the traditional teaching.

About the particular teaching of "moral menace" and "judgment long deferred" there are a few things to say:

1   What sins is the Doctor referring to that deserve *massacre* as punishment? In fact, *there are no such sins* - none, which justify massacre. Massacre is always a crime against humanity. By the very deed, the perpetrator proves he (or she) is worse than his (or her) victims, even if the victims were bad. Massacre kills indiscriminately - but clearly, the indiscriminate nature of the punishment does not worry the advocates of this vile teaching. They are already inured to injustice in "the ways of God", from the teaching in The Ten Commandments. There, punishment on children for sins of parents goes on to the third and fourth generations (Ex 20 v 5), which, by then, would mean many, *many* people continuing to be punished for the sins (or, more likely, *non*-sins) of one! I have already mentioned exclusions to the *tenth* generation, later added to the law. Indiscriminate punishment is endemic in the Bible - even in The Ten Commandments. The whole popuation of Canaan is regarded as guilty of something so vile, they deserve a violent and merciless death - even young children and animals, two categories of living beings that are not *usually* branded "criminals", fit only for the death penalty!

All this should worry Christians. It worries normal people. What has put Christians so far outside the sphere of normal thinking that they can accept this evil in the teaching? It is very alarming to think that it has gone on for so long, without normal, moral judgments being applied.

Furthermore, massacre is the *worst* kind of warfare. It is *never justifiable,* yet the Good News Bible, one of the popular, modern translations, much used in churches and in schools, has, as its title to Numbers Chapter 31, an account of one of the many massacres, "Holy War against Midian". This is *shocking*, for it is one of the vilest chapters in the Bible, all fifty-four verses of it!

Even *if* the population of Canaan *were* guilty of something - and, are we not *all* guilty of something? - they were guilty of *no* crime against the Israelites. On the contrary, they deserved *thanks* for the kindness and hospitality shown to their forebears, whom they had allowed in from outside Canaan, and shared their land, living peaceably alongside them. They deserved thanks for all the food the invaders had been consuming for a year before the slaughter began on the *west* of the Jordan - it having alsready begun on the east. But no - the people who had cultivated the fields, grown the crops, tended the vines, dressed the olive trees, and dug the irrigation channels, were made to starve, and die of thirst, if not blades, when the "holy nation"came to do their Lord's vile bidding!

If traditionalists think there were no innocents among the massacred populations of Canaan, they are very much beyond the pale of the thinking of the ordinary person. And they are wrong; *they were all innocent.* Their only crime was to be living where the Israelites wanted to live - and that is *no* crime, *no* sin, and *no* "moral menace"!

2   The Doctor says that the physical presence of the Canaanites constituted a moral menace that could not be tolerated. Who is *he* to say so? He has evidently overlooked, also, what is plainly written all over the Bible record of the invasion, that, after Jericho, the female virgins were saved for the Israelite men. That means there must have been children born to Canaanite women. The very lechery of the Israelite men ensured that a physical Canaanite presence would remain amongst them! The moral menace was not to the Israelites - it was to the *Canaanites*!

Furthermore, it seems that Abraham's concubine, Keturah, was Midianite, as was Moses' wife, Zipporah. Ruth was Moabite, and Bathsheba, one of David's *many* wives, was probably Hittite, since her husband, Uriah, was. The kings of Israel were notorious for taking foreign women, *whether in marriage or not,* and the practice seems to have gone on throughout the population. In this tragic and unsavoury way, *some* Canaanite lives were saved, and their genes passed on into the future. Alas, there was *no* future for most of them!

The poor, long-suffering Israelite women had to put up with the constant infidelity of their men, and, as we might guess, their patience was never appreciated. A saying of the rabbis, of a later age, goes, "We can know who our mother is, but who can be sure who his father is?" Precisely! So much for the godliness of the Israelite men! This is typical of the derogatory attitude to women in the Bible, and an element, itself of the moral menace of the religion contained therein.

3   Why is idol-worship regarded as a moral menace, when it evidently did not inspire its followers to be anything other than kind, welcoming, hospitable people? Because the Israelites said so! Why should we believe them? We should not. We should use our own judgment, which usually tells us that we should *not* go along with the ideas of people who are able to justify murder, massacre and genocide.

4   If the God of Israel inspires murder, and on *such* a scale - should we not take from the Bible that idol-worship is *better,* since it does not? Of course!

If the idols do not inspire murder, they are automatically superior to gods who do - or a God that does. In fact, *any* creed that inspires murder must be inferior to any creed, say atheism, that does not.

5   The insinuation traditionally made in sermons, is that what was really wrong with "pagan" religion was that it contained temple prostitution. The preachers never seem to see that murder is worse than prostitution. They think that it justified the attempted elimination of the Canaanites. Luckily, ordinary people see that it does *not* justify it. The trick played in the Bible is to blame the other side, for Israel's own sexual sins. There are enough accounts of these, in the very Bible record, to enable us to see that *this* is what has happened here: they accused the opponent of their own crimes!

6   As a clincher to the accusations of "moral menace", the traditionalists always allude to the alleged sins of Sodom and Gomorrah. They would do well to remember that Sodom was a good enough place, with hospitable enough neighbours, for Lot and his family to choose to live there (Gen 31). Why go there if it was so bad? The answer is, "Because it was *not* so bad!" Certainly, Lot and his retinue were not massacred! The traditionalists would also do well to remember the Israelites of Gibeah, who, once they had massacred the native population there, and moved in, tolerated gang-rape, refusing to hand over for judgment, culprits who had murdered, in the course of it. That those calling for justice, in Judges 19, was a Levite, therefore a *priest*, backed up by eleven tribes, held no sway with these Israelites, of the tribe of Benjamin.

Israel's sins were such that she was in no position to criticize anyone - not the people of Sodom, nor yet the people of Gomorrah - *no one*! People can see that - ordinary people using their brains and their common sense are making better judgments than those blinded by indoctrination.

Why haven't our theologions used their brains and their common sense, likewise? After all, they are paid to think about those things! It can only be that it is cosier to stick to things already taught. To think differently is to risk being ostracized from the Establishment. Follow the party line, safe in the holy huddle, reiterating the same ancient ideas, with a bit of new jargon: "That'll keep the next lot of students happily trotting out the old ideas", is easier. Those self-styled guardians of morality have perpetuated ancient misunderstandings. That is how Judaism has gone on being taught in Christianity, when is it manifestly the *opposite* of what Christ taught and died for! The traditional teaching justifies the unjustifiable, and *that* is why the Church is failing. People's private judgments differ from the official teaching, so they leave. Some stay, clinging on to the bits of truth they can find, hoping the lies will be identified and thrown out. They are repelled by all the killing. The doctrines that inspired them, those of the Chose People and the Promised Land, must be got rid of.

Jesus learned Judaism from the teachers in the Temple and in the synagogue. We learn that he "turned that teaching upside down", calling the Scribes, Pharisees and Doctors of the law hypocrites, who were teaching the doctrines of *men*. He demonstrated how they made blasphemous laws, which made Heaven remote, even unattainable to the common man (Luke 11 v 46). His teaching elevated those despised by the Establishment, and claimed *they* were the ones God favoured.

Jesus took up the cause of the second-class citizen of his day, those descended from the Canaanites made slaves, as likely they were, and said God was with *them* (Matt 5). He condemned silly religion, with silly regulations, and rituals that did not make a person kind or good. He deliberately broke them, to demonstrate that true religion, as some of the prophets had tried to point out, is to work for justice, to show mercy, to care for the needy - in other words, it was a state of the heart, *not* a show of prayers and sacrifices. He demonstrated how the religious people constantly broke the laws they pretended to keep: The Ten Commandments condemned them, because they purported to keep them, whilst they killed without mercy, and without conscience - and on the Sabbath, when they would not lift a stick, they would plot murder.

Christianity teaches that life is not about being great, but about being good - but then is silent about the evil of the genocide of the Canaanites. This cannot be allowed to continue; the people are thinking. They now see that, contrary to the traditional teaching of the "moral menace" of the Canaanites, the reverse is true - the Canaanites represent the moral good. The moral pose of the Israelites was a sham, and certainly, *their* physical presence meant calamity for all who encountered them. The Israelites were the "moral menace"!

CHAPTER 9

THE PHILISTINES

QUESTION: What does the word "Philistine" mean?

ANSWER: Someone who despises beautiful things.   (TV Quiz Show)

There is double injustice in the meaning we have hung on the word "Philistine". Perpetual insult is heaped upon original injury. Instead of the quiz answer above, the dictionary definition *should* read, "Someone who suffers vicious and unprovoked attack".

Sadly, Christianity has spread far and wide the lie that the Philistines were bad people, who despised beauty, in the form of the Israelites and their culture. That this culture was death to all nations, who stood in the way of their plans, and death to their cultures, as well, does not seem to have been reflected on, in the Christian blindness of seeing only *one* side of the story, the teller's version.

Yet, the very opposite of the accepted definition of the word, is plainly to be discovered from the Bible text, when it is read with unblinkered eyes. The Philistines were civilised people, living happily in their land of Philistia, when the unruly Israelites arrived on their borders, determined to have *their* land next. Even the writer of Judges admits to their unruliness - see the last verse of that book. Not that he is complaining about the countless and untold atrocities against the indigenous people, although he must have known of plenty. No - he is responding to the Levite's protest to the eleven Israelite tribes, about the tribe of Benjamin's failure to bring to justice those responsible for the death of his concubine, his "property". The result of the refusal of that tribe to cooperate on the matter, resulted in civil war against Benjamin. Far from complaining about harm done to the native populations, the terrible deeds done to *them* are recorded as virtuous, even religious acts, with the self-righteous disdain that religious fanatics are wonderful at displaying. The exploits of Samson and David are testimony to that.

By contrast to the anarchy in Israelite society at that time, the Philistines were living peacefully, growing crops and looking after their families, allowing Israelites to live amongst them, even giving sanctuary to Israelite warriors, who were sworn enemies to them. *That* was how civilised the Philistines were, compared to the Israelites. I have written elsewhere about Samson and David, both of whom made the Philistines their particular target for attack. It was their *religion* that made them hate people who did not hate them, and fight nations who tried to live in peace with them, sharing the land. In this, the Philistines, like the Canaanites, were more liberal, and more civilized than many nations before or since. Yet, in the Christian Church, Samson is the hero *for killing Philistines*! This is monstrous. Likewise David is a Christian hero. Why? For killing Philistines! Christians have been *mad* to believe this teaching. How *could* they have gone along with it for so long? It is almost beyond belief that Christians can have accepted, and for so long, the vilification of the sweet, amenable, kind-to-a-fault Philistines, and perpetuated the myth of the genocidal invaders being full of holiness and morality!

The history of the Philistines was written by their attackers, unusually vicious attackers at that, who came, uninvited and unprovoked, to wage a war of attrition for their land. Yet, even though their story was written by their enemies, *still,* the light of the Philistines' superiority of culture and manners shines through the pages, to those who take off the dark glasses of indoctrination.

As a *political* policy, "We take your land, and kill you", is not usually regarded as ethical. The United Nations, as well as the Churches and other religions, usually denounce such policies, where they occur in the world, as they constantly still do. To pretend it is *religion*, and claim it is not politics, is not usually a good enough excuse, either, for taking someone's country. Territorial ambition is not *usually* equated with religion - with the exception of the Bible. Then, all common sense and all moral sense disappear from the scene, as Christians are taught that *in the Bible* such a policy is good and right! This lapse in logic is bad enough, the gap in moral thinking is much worse, but the chasm between morality and religion is devastating!

This chasm needs to be attended to. Did Christians ever believe their ministers who told them the Philistines were bad for not handing over their land to the Israelites? I know several people who reacted against this teaching from their Sunday School days, and never joined the Church. Others did join the Church, but sympathised with the Philistines. After all - where were they to go to, if they gave up their land voluntarily? If they *had* moved out, and killed the people of the next land, to move into it, would *that*, also, be doing God's will? People in Scotland see through the phoney logic of the Bible. They despise it - and they are quite right! Which Christians would move out of *their* homes, and make the Title Deeds over to an armed burglar, who said God gave it to him? What Christian nation would move off *its* territory, and give it to another that claimed it as its right from God? *None!* Nor should they.

In *no* other context would the story of such territorial conquest be called "good" and "right" by Christians - only in the Bible. Here, the innocent are called bad, and the guilty are called good, and it is accepted! *Unholy* Bible - *this* is what has happened in it - the truth is sneered at, and made out to be a lie, and the lie is made out to be the truth. And all the time, the religions claim to be interested in the truth, and *based* on the truth. How very, very devious! It is a *lie* that the Philistines did not appreciate beautiful things - the evidence is there in the Bible, albeit by default. The Philistines respected life, even to the extent of shielding their enemies, (see 1 Sam 21). They had *order* in their lives, living peacefully with their neighbours, until the Israelites came bringing war. They had a life-enhancing religion, until the "holy nation" came with death and destruction. Beauty was not presented to the Philistines in the Bible - what was presented to them was *ugliness,* the ugliness of false friends, greed, bigotry and racism. They are in no wise to blame for despising those things!

CHAPTER 10

THE PALESTINIANS

"Of course we sympathise with the suffering of the Jews in the Holocaust; but you cannot translate that into your own doom." (Edward Said in TV Interview)

The nativity plays, which children perform in churches and schools at Christmas time, regularly feature shepherds wearing pyjamas and towels, in an attempt to look Middle Eastern. Sometimes, one or two of the actors is able to acquire an Arab headdress, even a Palestinian *koffiyeh,* and this gives a look of authenticity to the piece performed. Certainly, Palestinian Christians think that their ancestors were the first people to receive the "good tidings of great joy", in the fields outside Bethlehem. Today, some sheep are kept there by Muslims, in honour of the Christian tradition.

So, were the shepherds in the fields not Jews, after all, but descendants of the original people, the Canaanites? It is certainly to be hoped that more Canaanites survived, than the Old Testament record leads us to believe. We read of a few survivors, who even served in the Israelite army. Changing sides did not help them to survive very long, however: Uriah the Hittite was sent to certain death by David, to hide his adultery with the former's wife, for she had conceived by it; and the Amalekite, who brought him news of Saul's death, was summarily executed for his pains. Scholars think that many more Canaanites continued to live on in ancient Palestine than the Bible would have us believe, that the accounts of wholesale slaughter are much exaggerated - the wishful thinking of the authors. Let us hope so - the wishful thinking is bad enough!

If the shepherds in the fields at the time of Jesus' birth were not descendants of Canaanites, why were they not? It could only be because they had all been killed off in Old Testament times. If a few survived, and tragically, it could only have been a few, they were perhaps the descendants of the Hittites of Gibeon, made slaves by Israel, eventually becoming that part of the society outside the religion proper, the Sinners. In this class there would also be the descendants of mixed parentage, when the Israelite men took the Canaanite virgins. As such, they would never be accepted as belonging to "the Lord's people", yet *those* were the ones befriended by Jesus. By Jesus' day, their origins would have become obscured, being just the underclass in Jewish society, and not consciously Canaanite or part-Canaanite.

The conquest of Canaan is reckoned to have taken about three hundred years. At any point, the Israelites could have stopped, and settled amongst the surrounding nations, but no right was ever accorded others to live on their own lands. It *had* to be domination. Treaties and contracts never conferred equal rights on the other party involved, as Gen 34 v 24 shows, even in a marriage contract. The whole tribe of Dinah's husband had to be circumcised, and become Hebrews (before they were slain). And even *after* the law was given to "love thy neighbour as thyself", it was primarily meant for Israelite neighbours - and only later extended to *individual* foreigners, living amongst them - never to the Canaanite or Philistine tribes around, who were never accorded the right to *live*. This was right-wing politics like we have seldom seen in respectable society - the mentality of Hitler and Stalin before their time. And the Hebrews claimed they were - not *just* respectable society, but the model for all others for all time - "a light to lighten the gentiles"!

So, Philistine and Canaanite blood, *if* any continued to flow in veins down the generations, would be in the Jewish underclass, called "Sinners". Most of these would have become Christians in the time of Jesus, whose message to them was so much more positive than the current religion's. The Palestinians see themselves as the descendants of the Philistines, and the territory in Roman times was named after them, Palestine. Thus the line of some of the ancient inhabitants continued to live in their original land.

Unfortunately, the guilt-ridden Allies of the Second World War, who, in the United Nations, in 1947, voted for a plan to divide up Palestine between Arabs and Jews, did not feel *enough* guilt. Their guilt only extended to Hitler's atrocious treatment of the Jews. There were, and are, many other victims, not given much sympathy, or help, or even thought. There should have been guilt about the broken promise, to the Palestinians, of self-rule, in return for helping the Allies in the First World War to oust the Turks from Palestine. The promise was broken, even as it was being made, by the Balfour Declaration of 1917. This document, promising a homeland for the Jews in Palestine, must have been in preparation at the very time the Allies were making the promise of autonomy to the Palestinians, for the text of the Declaration was ready, even before the Turks had left Jerusalem, in *December* 1917. Money and titles spell *influence* in the world of politics, and the Zionist Movement, which had been growing in Europe since the 1870s, had *both* - particularly the Rothschild barons. There was so much Jewish influence behind the scenes in the British Government, that it had already *offered*, in a letter from Lord Robert Cecil to

Chaim Weizmann, leader of the Zionist Movement, in the *spring* of 1917, *to be the protecting power of world Jewry in Palestine*! Weizmann has even gone on record as saying he *asked* Britain for a Jewish State, *and got it*!

By 1947, when Britain announced it was ending its Mandate in Palestine, it had come to realise the error of its ways. It abstained in the vote in the UN, on the partitioning of Palestine, with separate Jewish and Palestinian States, knowing that it spelled terrible trouble. The Arabs had coexisted peacefully with the first Jews who came to settle there, and some Jews had always lived there; but the large influxes, which were taking place in the first half of the twentieth century, were putting too much pressure on the land. There was not enough of it to go round! But the Allies were still reeling from the revelations of Hitler's savage slaughter of Jews and others, in concentration camps and gas chambers, during the war. They decided to ease their consciences by giving the Jews the homeland they wanted in Palestine.

Had not the Christian Church kept and taught, for two thousand years, the unchristian doctrines of a Chosen People and a Promised Land (this *Odium Theologicum)*, the handing over of 52% of Palestine - and the best, the most fertile part, at that - to another nation, to dominate the indigenous people, could not have been countenanced. But the European nations had had five hundred years of sailing around the world, seizing other people's lands, dividing up lands and people, often killing them, to the point of the extermination - remember the Native Americans, of both North and South, and remember the Australian Aboriginees and the Tasmanians, and others - they were not going to balk at giving little Palestine away! After all - they were giving the Promised Land back to God's Chosen People, were they not?

If it was such a godly thing to do - give away someone else's land - following the biblical example of the Old Covenant, presumably Britain would not have found it necessary to abstain, in the vote on the setting up of Israel in Palestine. In fact, logically speaking, if it was such a godly thing to do, then *all* the countries of the UN would have been offering *their* countries, dispossessing themselves. One could have thought that the USA might have thought it could atone, a little bit, for its own disgraceful treatment of the native people of its land, by offering some of the USA to "God's cause"! (*Not* that *that* would have helped the native peoples!) But that did not happen. *No* nation came rushing to sacrifice itself for the cause of "the Lord's Chosen People" - and so the Palestinians were sacrificed. And the USA, famous for killing off the indigenous people, and then pleading for population saying, "Give us your poor", would not even allow in the number of Jews who applied for entry!

The Palestinians were totally innocent of the Holocaust, yet, they are the ones who are paying the price for it. *They* are Hitler's latest victims. The Church, which , although unwittingly and indirectly, brought about this situation, must not stay silent any longer, allowing this monstrous situation to continue unchallenged. The Church must rethink its erroneous doctrines, and apologise for getting some of them *so* wrong for *so* long.

It is inexcusable that, more than fifty years after the end of the Second World War, after suffering massacres, attacks, tricks and hounding, and United Nations edicts to get them out of their homes and off their land, thousands of Palestinians are still living in refugee camps, and are refugees in other countries. The patience and long-suffering of this nation went unnoticed by the West, blinded by the false Old Testament doctrines in Christianity, that the land was rightfully the Jews'. No - it was rightfully that of the people born there, just as it was when Abraham first saw it, and when Moses looked at it from across the Jordan. Three thousand years ago the Israelites took it by terrorism and genocide, and in the twentieth century, their descendants again took it by terrorism, even while the western nations were trying to *give* it to them!

Existence for the Palestinians is made ever more wretched by the Israelis, who impose huge restrictions on their daily lives. What they are allowed to do, even in the areas called "self-governing", is only what the Israelis *allow* them to do. Life for the Palestinians of Gaza and the West Bank is made ever more difficult, as more Palestinian land continues to be seized, and turned into Settlements for Israelis from abroad, with roads linking Settlements cutting through mature Palestinian olive groves, and cutting Palestinian communites off from each other, leaving them isolated, like tiny islands in an Israeli sea. Water is rationed to the Palestinians, and often cut off; jobs are denied them, prosperity from tourism is syphoned off by the Israelis. In short, the Palestinian economy is deliberately sabotaged, and by many devious means. The underlying idea must be to starve them out of the country.

The Jews pose for ever as victims of the Holocaust, planning museums all over Britain, to commemorate it, whilst they are the ones who originated a Holocaust on Canaan, yet not a word is ever said about that! Palestinians are suffering from that holocaust today, as Israel tries to repeat the history of three thousand years ago, just a bit more subtly. They still insult *all* foreigners by deigning to call a few "righteous gentiles" - which infers that all others are *unrighteous*. This self-righteous attitude permeates the law in Israel, which, whilst regarding itself as civilised, violates the human and civil rights of the indigenous people of the land where they live, the Palestinians.

The saintly Elias Chacour, in his book, BLOOD BROTHERS, evidently sees the usurpers of his land in a very different light from the way they see him. "Brother children of Abraham"is not how the Israeli settlers choose to see him or his compatriots. As I said in the previous chapter, I do not believe the Palestinians are descended from Abraham - doubtless some are - but there is another important point: Palestinians do not require kinship in order to be hospitable and caring - that is their nature anyway. We see it in the Bible, in the ways of the Philistines. The Canaanites were like that before ever Abraham came to the land, for he *found* the people like that! The Palestinians are like that. Neither do they insult the rest of us, by calling *a few "righteous gentiles"*, but treat *all* people well. It is their nature, and their culture.

Some readers may be surprised, even incredulous, at my view of a people, whose name, "Palestinian", in the 1970s, became almost synonymous with "terrorist". Indeed, in their despair at their plight being ignored on the world stage, some *did* resort to terrorism. It would be good to say that terrorists never do their cause any good, for right-thinking people are put off the cause of any terrorist. I *wish* I could say that. Certainly, Palestinians have all suffered, because of the terrorist activities of a few, both in world opinion, and through the clampdowns on the whole of the West Bank and Gaza, with curfews, arbitrary arrests, torture whilst in custody, road closures, removal of travel passes and increased travel restrictions. I know that terrorism did not come easily to the Palestinians, for they are peace-loving by nature. I can only think that some were *driven* to terrorism, in their despair, and I feel very sorry for them.

It would be a good thing to say, "all terrorists are bad people, for they are small groups, who are determined to impose their will on others by force, paying no heed to the wishes of the majority of people, nor to the democratic way of the ballot box". Yet, even in this tragic area of life, it is not possible to say that, for some *governments* are terrorist, and the outside world is not always willing, or able, to help the downtrodden.

Nelson Mandela wrote very movingly on this issue in his autobiography, LONG WALK TO FREEDOM. He explains it thus:

"We had no alternative to armed and violent resistance. Over and over again, we had used all the non-violent weapons in our arsenal - speeches, deputations, threats, marches, strikes, stay-aways, voluntary imprisonment - all to no avail, for whatever we did was met by an iron hand. A freedom fighter learns the hard way, that it is the oppressor who defines the nature of the struggle, and the oppressed is often left no recourse but to use methods that mirror those of the oppressor. At a certain point, one can only fight fire with fire."

Terrible violence was done to the Palestinian people, and the Christian West took no notice - even worse, it tacitly assented to the violence against peaceful, unarmed Palestinians, because it had accepted the violence against the Canaanites in its holy book. Christianity made the protests of *individual* Christians weak, for Christianity teaches that Palestine was the land God promised to the Jews. In the old South Africa, the Church world-wide could see the injustice and evil of Apartheid - but the Church has never been able to see the injustice and evil of Zionism. I would expect anyone to be driven *mad* by such callous neglect,and it is no wonder to me that some Palestinians took to terrorism. The Church should feel guilty for ignoring their cries for help. It should have been at the forefront of trying to right the wrongs done to the Palestinians.

The world should also remember that oppressed people are damaged people, who need help and understanding. Those who are daily at the sharp end of brutality cannot be expected to think in the calm way of the academic. The attitude required is that shown by Dickens towards the savagery of the French, in their Revolution of 1789. In A TALE OF TWO CITIES, he shows compassion and understanding of their crimes, in the character of a young seamstress, obviously innocent of any crime, waiting to be guillotined. Ironically, by her words, she shows that she is a supporter of the Revolution, who is totally confused by what is happening to her; and even though it is putting her to death, she continues to believe in it;

"If the Republic really does good to the poor, and they become less hungry, and in all ways to suffer less, she (her relative) may live a long time; she may even live to be old."

The patience and forbearance of the Palestinians needs to be appreciated by the West, and especially, by the Church. Who, reading this, could have been *half* so generous, loving and forgiving, in the face of such suffering and oppression, as they have been?

CHAPTER 11

RELIGION

"He (Jesus) frees us from religion." (THE SHAKING OF THE FOUNDATIONS by Paul Tillich)

We are at a point in this book where we really need to consider the question, "What is this thing called religion?" Is it something that answers a *need* in us, which most religions say is *God*? Is it a set of beliefs we have learned, and assent to - a *creed*? Is it our *view* of the world, which we may, or may not, be able to express in words?

There are many different definitions of what religion is, and we can take our pick of them. My own view is that religion is the answer to a longing we have within us - a yearning for the ideal world, with a need to be loved, and to feel we belong, being part of this longing. Tied up with this longing, there is a knowledge within, our conscience, which enables us to recognise the good we long for. Religion should, therefore, automatically bring us a feeling of satisfaction and of completeness, that we could not have without it, giving us a reason to sing and dance with joy! The feelings accompanying the finding of our religion - with our biggest questions answered, our biggest fears removed, our hunger within satisfied - should all be positive ones. Low spirits should soar high.

Probably devotees, in all religions, would say that their religion does those things for them. So far so good! As Jesus promised in his Sermon on the Mount (Matt 5), the meek are blessed, those who mourn are comforted. This is no mean thing, for the world is full of suffering, and people are crying out for help and comfort. Sometimes their only comfort is in God. What other comfort is there for parents who have lost a child? What other comfort is there for fear of death? What other comfort is there for those ravaged by war, incurable physical or mental disease or disability, injustice, or by the criminal activity of wicked people? There are many situations in life, where there can be no other comfort, except that God knows, God sees, and God will right wrongs.

Some people regard this as wishful thinking. Well - that is interesting, if it is reckoned to be everybody's wish. I do not think it is just wishful thinking. The universe is known to be *much* more amazing than anyone in the world could possibly have dreamt. It is vaster than our minds can comprehend. Life is more intricate than any of us would ever have imagined, without science telling us so. Every day we learn, and discover more that was unimaginable and unimagined, through science. Doubtless, there is more to know, that science, *wonderful* as it is, cannot discover. Most of what Jesus taught makes wonderful sense to me. I find the code of *love* makes most sense to live by. *Duty* is too cold. *Blind obedience* to a dictator is too dangerous, for he could be wrong. Even if he started off well, he might go off the rails, giddy with power. The kind of love that is *"Do as you would be done by",* is the creed that would transform the world into the place we would like it to be. It fits in with the petition in the prayer Jesus taught, "Thy will be done on Earth, as it is in Heaven."

How is it, though, that religion, which should be a force for so much good, has actually emanated so much bad, by way of arrogance, tyranny, fear, threats, curses, cruel punishments, massacre - as we have seen in previous chapters? One reason is that it becomes stunted and unhealthy when it is inward-looking. Concentrating on personal or national goals, it becomes self-centred, and therefore, selfish. Some devotees become so dedicated to what they see as personal holiness that they put up with all sorts of misery, "mortification of the flesh", as St Paul calls it. They can also be a real pain to those around them! Jesus gave the antidote to this in the challenge, "Love your neighbour as yourself". This does not sound like an injunction to put oneself through unnecessary pain, as some people do, in acts like self-flageolation, for it could never be right to do that to others!

In fact, Jesus was quoting the religion of his upbringing, for these very words come from Leviticus 19 v 18. But there, "neighbour" referred only to fellow-Israelites - certainly not Canaanites. Jesus extended the scope of this verse, to refer to everyone in the world. In the parable to illustrate the answer to the question, "But who *is* my neighbour?" he made the despised foreigner, the man of doubtful race, and even more doubtful religion, the Samaritan, the hero (Luke 10). "Love your neighbour as yourself" becomes, then, a challenge to religion itself, which should prevent it from becoming inward-looking, smug, exclusive. That simple maxim is the perfect religion, in tune with heart and conscience, understandable even to young children.

But those verses, quotations and parables are well-known, so how is it that Christianity continues to have less and less impact on young people, even as they search for meaning and purpose in life? How is it that Christianity speaks with conflicting voices, and continues to dwindle in number?

I set forth my view. Instead of a religion of *heart and conscience,* in tune with God, Christianity chose to become "a religion of the Book". Unfortunately, the Book has proved, not only difficult to understand, but to speak with many different massages, some of them contradictory, like "love your neighbour" and "kill the Canaanites". To fail to admit this, means that it is certainly going to be misunderstood. Most of this book is of, and for, the Hebrew nation, being their early history - with embellishment and bias - their literature, and their religion. It is offensive to other nations, bigoted and racist - and the Christian Church has inflicted it on its members for nearly two thousand years!

Christianity is, therefore, a hotch-potch of Old Testament bigotry and New Testament confusion. Jesus' wonderful new, dazzling message of love and peace has been hijacked into a stereotypical religion of olden form, instead of what it *should* have been - the *release* from old-style religion! Christians are sick of the double-speak. There is hate, where there is supposed to be love, and it is not just in the Old Testament. Church members have given up trying to make sense of it, and stay away, discouraged. Many of them would like to return to Church, for they are attracted to Jesus, and his teaching of love and peace - but they are past being fooled by false platitudes. They notice when the last verse is conveniently omitted, in the reading of Psalm 137, "Babylon, you will be destroyed. Blessed is he who repays you for what you have done to us, who takes your infants, and smashes them against a stone." This is *disgusting*. How are people supposed to accept that this was written by a "man after God's own heart"? In fact, Babylon, from the Bible record, treated the writer's people *a thousand times better* than they ever treated any of the nations they came across!

No, most Christians are *not* comfortable that such words and such sentiments can be in a book called "holy", being expressed by people called "holy", and they would like some answers as to how the Church justifies this. Yet, there are some, often called Fundamentalists, who seem able to reconcile all the irreconcilables in the book. They are able to do the mental contortions required, in order to see no discrepancies. They are able to accept the whole book as the Word of God, blindly accepting the doctrines of the Chosen People and the Promised Land. They are happy with New Testament references to Hell, and happy with Old Testament mass-murderers being hailed as Christian heroes. This is fearful! These I would call "Old Testament Christians", inured to the traditional beliefs, used to the confusion, and unwilling to question what their forefathers handed on to them. To question might turn their world upside down - but they do need to question, especially, why a religion of death and destruction is in the midst of a religion which is supposed to be about peace and love.

The message of the angel to the shepherds of Bethlehem was of "peace on Earth, goodwill to all mankind". Peace is not just the absence of war. True peace is based on justice for everyone. "Love your enemy" sounds like a contradiction in terms, for Christians should not have enemies. However, one only has to remember that the Israelites of the Old Testament went around making enemies out of friends. It may "take two to tango", but sadly, it takes only one belligerent person to start a fight, as we saw in Chapter 4. An imposed peace is not true peace, for war will always be liable to break out. Goodwill has to be present, for then there is a will for *justice*, the basis of true peace.

Instead of concentrating on being a religion of heart and mind and ideals - of peace and goodwill - Christianity became a copy-cat religion. The Church of Scotland is *proud* to tell that it modelled its services, originally, on the synagogue service. By becoming a religion of a "holy book" - and *such* a book , containing a religion of death and destruction, war and hate, side by side with a religion that contradicts all that - it sank into the mire of trying to make the ungodly godly! In additon, it bogged itself down with with set forms and traditions that were totally unnecessary to it. Some Old Testament type of Christians still want to add more! I heard one say on the radio that Christianity should have an equivalent to the Jewish Feast of Purim, that celebration of massacre throughout the Persian Empire during the time of The Exile!

Christianity was meant to free us from all that. Jesus' injunction, "Go and preach the gospel all over the world", was meant to *liberate* people from the stranglehold of fear and superstition, from the domination of despotic religious leaders, corrupted by the power they wielded over the masses, imposing their will, and keeping alive traditions, however burdensome or unedifying they were, insisting they could not be changed - for change might mean diminution of their power. Instead of experiencing that liberating kind of Christianity, for generation after generation, the Church has bogged people down with the history of the Hebrew nation from nearly 2000BC - a history and religion we did not need to know, nor want to know - so that our very literature, over hundreds of years is threaded through and through with it! What an imposition of one line of one man's dream, ambition and determination upon the rest of us! What unedifying stuff! We *might* have learned something more edifying - and more enjoyable!

If it had even taught us good things! But, tragically, it taught an ancient killer-God, who loved his followers to kill. Because the Church did not *correct* this message, with the message of brotherly love, but *incorporated it into* its message, it bred Christians and Christian nations who emulated the undesirable part of the mixed message. They justified their arrogance from it, and justified their actions form it. Thus, *so-called* Christian nations sailed out from Europe, plundering and conquering territory, thinking it was all right to mistreat others, abuse them, even kill them... The trouble with not learning the correct lessons from history, or *religion,* is that we will then repeat the errors!

It was bad enough that *secular* society produced armies and navies that went around the world, visiting all sorts of indignities upon defenceless populations. Far worse was that the Church *itself* did this, taking the idea of "holy war" straight from the Old Testament. To be fair to the Israelites, it took Moses and Joshua much longer to turn them into a killing machine - the Bible says forty years - than it took Pope Urban III, in 1095, and subsequent popes, to turn the medieval Church into the same. One speech by His Holiness was enough to raise a rapacious, massacring army, every bit as vicious as that of Moses and Joshua. Had the Church paid attention to the teaching of Jesus, no such wars as the Crusades could ever have been waged. "Let the wheat and tares grow together", he taught. Well, people of different nationalities and different religions, were living peacefully in Jerusalem, side by side, threatening no one, when the Crusaders came to massacre them. Ironically, and disgracefully, the unchristlike armies of an unchristlike Church, went emblazoned with the Cross, symbol of the Man of Peace. Such irony is not unusual; doubtless Abraham said "Shalom" to everyone he hoped to denude of their land!

But the Church declared "holy war", justifying the unjustifiable, and setting the scene for all the subsequent marauding forces of the greedy kings and queens of Christendom, which went rampaging around the world, looting and plundering for the next nine hundred years, until the oppressed fought back. No wonder people in the West have turned against religion in a big way - instead of teaching peace, it taught war; instead of teaching love, it taught hate; instead of displaying the humility of a forgiven people, who knew they were sinners, it fostered the arrogance of a "chosen people", calling themselves "elect", in the words of St Paul; instead of being a vehicle of healing and wholeness, it administered a poisoned chalice, which ruined individual lives, the lives of nations, and international relations. The effects of this evil doctrine of Holy War are incalculable; they are *still* reverberating in the Middle East, where the people regard the Crusades as continuing to this day, with the State of Israel being the latest phase of Western conquest.

The only remedy for this is for Christianity to jettison the theology of the Old Covenant. The God of death and war are its teaching. Its heroes are villains, who terrorised and murdered. Since they are also venerated as heroes in the New Testament, it will have to be examined in a new light, to see exactly which parts are, and which are not, in keeping with the teaching of Jesus. The list in Hebrews 11 can no longer be tolerated as men of faith, in the Christian sense. Christian theologians will be reluctant to do this, for it means rethinking, and it means upheaval, with ramifications unclear, and outcomes unknown; far easier, and safer, to trot out the old cliches, as they have done for two thousand years.

But regurgitating the old food will no longer do. Church members are thinking and questioning, and the old platitudes no longer satisfy. If Jesus is the Bread of Life, let the food be served without poison in it; if Jesus is the Truth, let theologians end the lies; if Jesus the Way to God, let us hear what that means, without telling us that we need to assent to vicious doctrines in a confused, and confusing book!

A cleansed Christianity is what we need for the 21st century - cleansed from the wicked God of evil deeds, and from wicked heroes. Just as Judaism is without Christianity, Christianity needs to be without Judaism.

CHAPTER 12

THE EFFECT OF CHRISTIANITY ON MIDDLE EAST POLITICS

"It was in Tennessee that I first learned about the history of my native land, in partition-divided Sunday School rooms, covered with pictures and maps of the Holy Land. Before I was six, I had walked through Judaea, Galilee, Capernaum, Bethlehem, Jerusalem, sharing a dusty road with Jesus and the disciples... Over these hills and desert places, my forebears - Abraham, Isaac, David and Solomon - had roamed, killing the enemies of the Lord, and establishing a kingdom for the children of promise."   (TO A DANCING GOD by Sam Keen)

Although Sam Keem wrote these words thirty years ago, and in the USA, my experience of Sunday School in Scotland was similar - as it is for Christian children all over the world, even today.   Christian children were brought up, here also, to identify with the Israelites of the Old Testament, even to see themselves as part of the family of Abraham, inheritors of his faith! The same mish-mash of Old and New Testaments is dished up still, in Church and Sunday School, to confuse and perplex any child who actually *thinks* about the incompatible values. Our literature and our music, our whole culture is laced with Bible references, texts and stories, told with the bias of the writers, unexamined and uncriticised. Fortunately, not so many people in Scotland, nowadays, are quite so prepared to do the psychological jiggery-pokery that traditional Christian teaching requires, and are questioning the motives for all the killing.

To the credit of the Church of Scotland, it never suggested to us that the Jews were to blame for the death of Jesus. Our ministers were always at pains to tell us that the Jews were *not* to blame - that , in fact , it was *our own sin* that put Jesus on the cross: *we* were to blame. Pontius Pilate was not usually blamed either: mostly, the line taken was "he was doing his best, in a difficult situation". Only the occasional Church sermon slated him. I was therefore, very surprised to hear, when I was in France in the 1960s, that the then Pope, had publicly blamed the Jews for crucifying Jesus. (This view has recently been rescinded by the present Pope.) It had never been part of the Christianity I learned, to blame the Jews. I mention this here, because I have heard rabbis, on British radio, say that Christianity teaches that the Jews were to blame for crucifying Jesus. *Not so:* I was taught that the Jews were, and are still (Romans 11) God's Chosen People. The larger part of Christian sacred scripture is Jewish.

The anti-Jewish feeling that arose in Germany in the 1930s, wherever it came from, cannot have come from the Church, unless it was teaching *very* different things from the Church in Scotland. In fact, Christianity is so Zionist that I wonder how any Palestinian can be Christian. Yet many are. I can only think that, to Palestinian Christians, the teaching is very different from the teaching in Scotland - or in the USA, or Africa, or everywhere - by all accounts! How can Palestinians be Christians, if God gave away their land - *twice*?

Paradoxically, the former Israeli Prime Minister, Benyamin Netanyahu, on British TV, accused Christianity of being anti-Jewish! Deliberately confusing it with Nazism, he said, "Christianity was responsible for the Holocaust against the Jews. You are in no position to criticize what we do!" This was always his ploy to allow no criticism of any of his right-wing policies, particularly that of taking more and more Palestinian land, and building more and more Settlements. It is true that Germany was, and is, a Christian country, but, I repeat, on my understanding of Christianity, the Holocaust could not have stemmed from this religion, even with the Old Testament war ethic! The Christianity I learned was always pro-Jewish.

In my view, Christianity is to blame for the disastrous situation in the Middle East today. The Church created a climate, world-wide, which supported Zionism, the movement whose aim was to create a Jewish State in Palestine. The Church had indoctrinated people, all over the world, to believe that this must be "of God", and therefore *right*, and so stood idly by, and even *assented* when hundreds of Jewish terrorists, in 1948, seized Palestine, massacring many hundreds of the indigenous population, and causing untold grief and loss to those who survived. *The Bible had shown that this was all right to do!* This must discredit the Bible completely. Protests from the Arab nations at the United Nations were of no avail - the USA had an evil vote, the *veto*, and used it time and time again to thwart any concerted action against the new Israel.

The unprotesting nations would not have countenanced their own territories being seized, and their people massacred - but it was all right if it was done by the Jews against the Palestinians - and *that is shocking*! This belief, that the Jews could do no wrong , came from Christianity. Yet, if the same attack had happened to Christian countries, they would never had believed that these were God's people, carrying out God's will. They would have argued that the very level of violence used, proved it was *not* God's will - although that is not an argument they could sustain from the Bible! Then they voted for an Israeli State, anyway. Lucky for them Abraham did not walk through *their* countries four thousand years ago: their situation would now be the same as that of the Palestinians!

In addition, Christianity has given Israel the huge success it has had in armed attacks for more land seizures, because Israel and its war machine, is largely financed from the USA. It is because those taxpayers were indoctrinated young with the doctrines of the Chosen People and the Promised Land - that and "the Jewish lobby" - that they meekly assent to this dreadful misuse of US taxpayers' money.

Christianity has kept, from the Old Testament, the metaphor of Mount Zion, a hill in Jerusalem, as the place where God lives, and therefore, a picture of Heaven, even a foretaste of Heaven on Earth. References to Zion permeate the New Testament and Christian hymns - thus many Christians look to Jerusalem, dreaming of prophecy and fulfilment. They even managed to see the 1967 War as fulfilling Old Testament prophecy, and as a step in the achievement of their New Testament dream, not clearly spelled out, but hazily presented, in the unfathomable book of Revelation. Some beguiled Christians, in many parts of the world, have been told that this is all part of God's plan for the world, seeing Israel to be "God's timepiece", as Colin Chapman describes in his book, WHOSE PROMISED LAND? They pray for Israel (but not Palestine), and look in the Bible for prophecies they can apply to the things the Israeli Government does. They find prophecies which were about a political situation two and a half thousand years ago, which they misapply to Israel now. They look in the book of Revelation, and they find whatever they want.

Had not Christianity imbued Christians with the ridiculous idea, taken straight from the Old Testament, that God gave the Hebrew nation the land of Canaan - and worse, that he gave them the right to kill all the inhabitants of that land, if they did not run away first - the Western nations would never have *thought* of putting Palestinians off their land, and giving it to the Jews, in the twentieth century. Had not Hitler, leader of a Christian nation, caused the unimagined horrors of the death camps and gas chambers of the Holocaust, the guilt, the sympathy of the Western nations might not have been quite so ready to ride rough-shod over the rights and aspirations of the Palestinian people in their own land, and vote in the UN in 1948 to dispossess hundreds of thousands of them of their homes, their livelihoods, their cities and villages - in fact, their country and their lives. On the very day that the British ended their Mandate in

67

Palestine, on 14 May, 1948, at midnight, Jewish terrorists declared a State of Israel, massacred hundreds of Palestinians in their villages, and evicted others from their towns and villages, making refugees of them.

Had not Christianity, with its evil Chosen People and Promised Land doctrines, dulled the minds of the Western nations to the violations of the human, civil and political rights of the Arab population, desperate Palestinians would not have felt they had to resort to terrorism, in order be noticed by the world, which was ignoring them. Terrorism is evil, but was it not the evil doctrines from the Old Testament that brought these other evils about? I think it was. Violence begets violence; evil begets evil. The false doctrines in Christianity brought about a climate of widespread assent to, and even support for, the terrorist State of Israel, which added to the despair of the Palestinians. In their despair, some followed the example of those who had been so successful. Christianity did not *mean* all this to happen, nor foresee it, but, because it cherished evil teaching, evil has resulted - and more will result, as surely as night follows day, if it does not rid itself of its false doctrines.

Not only in this century, but all down the ages, because Christianity failed to condemn the terrorism of the Old Testament, but instead, chose to base its doctrines on it, the course of history has been more violent than it should have been. Instead of teaching that terrorism was always wrong, it taught that terrorism could be right - *was* right in Canaan, and - could it be that it was also right in *Palestine*? The question is rhetorical - it is only to demonstrate the wickedness of the logic that follows from the false teaching! No wonder our history has been so violent! The Church practised terrorism in the Crusades. Christian nations practised terrorism in their colonising exploits. And only *now*, are Christian nations beginning to think that what is going on in Palestine does not seem to be very godly! It is no thanks to the Church that people are beginning to think differently, but to the Palestinians, who, at long last, and against many odds, are beginning to get their message out of the prisons and refugee camps, and into some of our newspapers, and on to our TV screens. Ordinary people are away ahead of the Church, in realising that the Palestinians have been greatly wronged, and, so late in the day as this, the Church, too, is beginning to see it. The war ethic of the Church, straight from the Old Testament, has caused incalculable suffering in the Middle East alone over the past nine hundred years.

Probably every nation has a guilty past. We are not to blame for the guilt of our forebears, but we *are* to blame if we fail to condemn wrong that was done, and to say we are sorry. We are also to blame if we do not try to put right that wrong, as far as is possible. In the case of Christianity, the Church must admit to its mistaken doctrines, which have led to bloodshed in the past, and which have led them to fail to support the downtrodden and oppressed people in the land of Jesus' birth, the very people whose cause Jesus espoused. The very *worst* thing is what the Church did in the past - *glorify* invasion, seizure, terror and genocide, as good, inspired by God, and "holy". The Church must repent of its mistakes and misdeeds, and implement its repentance by correcting them.

Just as a sound building cannot be built on faulty foundations, the Church cannot be strong on the basis of erroneous doctrine. Peace can only come in the Middle East when the terrorism of the Old Testament is admitted by the Church, and by Israel, to be just that - *terrorism,* and *not* "Holy War, *evil* and *not* good, *man's greed* and *not* God' grace. *Morality* has to be the foundation of any religion, and immorality must be condemned.. Only then does peace become possible, for peace must be founded on *justice.* If it is not, it is *oppression.*

The Church must relinquish the war ethic. To get Christianity on to the foundation of peace that Jesus advocated, should be the first priority for Christianity in the twenty-first century. Only upon the *peace ethic* can justice be constructed, and *justice* should permeate everything the Church teaches and does. There can be no justice for the Canaanites of old, for they are dead, but it would be fitting for the Church, who ignored them for so long - sometimes even *vilified* them - to state publicly that they should never have been attacked, oppressed or killed, that their land should *not* have been taken from them in God's name, that to say that God ordered what happened to them is blasphemy. Furthermore, the Church should set up monuments, at all identifiable places of slaughter, that it can gain permission for, recording the Canaanite names, and its repentance for failing to deplore their genocide sooner.

It must declare *repentance* for the Crusades, and not just the "regret" of hitherto. Likewise, it should set up monuments that publish its repentance, at all known sites of bloodshed and atrocity, all across Europe, and right through to Jerusalem. But it needs to do *more* than that, and turn its wealth into places of healing and wholeness on such sites, building hospitals and workshops to be owned and run by local people. The Church owes a huge debt to the Palestinians, for *they* are bearing the brunt of the Church's false teaching on "The Promised Land". It is *their* land in question, and they should rightfully have it. The Church

69

should state that this is so, in unequivocal terms. This is not "engaging in politics", it is correcting past misstatements, and correcting its doctrines. It is the two religions of Judaism and Christianity, which have caused the trouble in the Middle East that we see today. But for these, peace would have reigned there three thousand years ago, and should still be reigning there today. No such luck for that region - two *religions* have caused the past and present havoc!

What effect would this repentance, and saying "Sorry", have on the Palestinians? *Being* sorry is a bad feeling, but *saying* "Sorry" - and *meaning* it - begins a healing process, both in the penitent and in the wronged victim. *Both* begin to feel better, and come closer in mind. A repentant Church can be assured of having, at least, a better collective conscience, and less confusion in its beliefs about God. Palestinians, as the latter victims of Hitler's Holocaust, and Western guilt about it, can begin to experience *some* relief for the legacy of anger, disappointment, vexation and frustration, that really must have been *unbearable* this past half century. This will begin to become bearable, when sympathy and support become a reality for them. It is to be hoped they will forgive the Church for past crimes against them, as the Church asks for their forgiveness, and shows its repentance by implementing moral doctrines, not immoral, and by striving to make up for past wrongs.

The Palestinians are a living example of our saying, "hope springs eternal", for they have gone on hoping, in the face of an intransigence on the part of the Israelis that would blow apart the goodwill of all but the most patient of people. I am stunned with admiration at their willingness to go on listening, to go on trying to negotiate, trying to bargain, and to go on hoping, when they are met by constant double-talk, double-dealing and disparagement on the part of the key party. They are still hopeful, as they await developments in a new phase in the "Peace Process", with the new Israeli Prime Minister, Ehud Barak. Even as they wait, their land continues to be stolen, new Settlements begun, existing ones expanded, all on the Palestinians' land. No justice is possible for them, unless these Settlements are abandoned, and the land returned - but I fear that is not in Israeli thinking. Palestinian land, including East Jerusalem, continues to disappear from *their* hands into Israeli ones, by many different and devious means.

Yet, international condemnation of illegal land takeovers and Settlements continues to be muted, whilst the many human rights violations continue - blatant at Ben Gurion Airport, where the tourist population does not see how the Arabs are treated, when they are separated from the mainstream, and in other places where tourists do not go, such as the Identity Card Office for Arabs, where they are given forms to fill in, that are printed only in Hebrew - but sneaky and insidious, at places where outsiders might see. In Israeli prisons, torture, sometimes to death, of Palestinians is well-known, even admitted, and unapologised for.

Why is condemnation from other nations so muted? Apart from most of the crimes being unknown abroad, another important reason is the predisposition of Westerners to approve of everything Israel does. It was always proclaimed from church pulpits that Israel was "The Chosen Race". Everything they did was God's working out of his plan for the world. That should make him a monster of the first order! Sensible people realised that, and left the Church - or did not join, in the first place. To others of us, who sang, from a young age, "Christ was born in Bethlehem", we pictured it as a heavenly place. Everything *must* be wonderful there! The emergence of Israel in the post-war era was seen, in the Church, to be God at work in history (again). Church groups went from Scotland to visit, and came back, ecstatic, about the magnificent "Holy Land". They toured Church Guilds showing slides of the fun they had, floating on the Dead Sea. They showed pictures of Galilee and of other "holy places" - the *stones* they worshipped! Those of us who did not go assumed that the people living in Bethlehem were *also* having a great time; *everyone* there must feel they were living in Heaven!

Then, the 1970s television News programmes gave us pictures of acts of terror carried out by Palestinians. This was a shock. We had hardly even *heard* of them before! We certainly had not been told of any injustices against them, and we categorised them as "wicked". Not only were they hurting innocent people, they were *fighting God's people*, so they must be completely bad! To criticise was easy - life was black and white: moral judgments were also easy, either right or wrong - people acted either for God or the Devil! That was another of the false teachings from Sunday School - life is *not* black and white, but many shades of grey. Moral issues, as well as political ones, are not so simple and straightforward. And who needs the Devil, when "God is portrayed as not living up to even the minimum moral ideals" (Prior)?

In the late 1980s, television reports showed pictures of the *Intifada*, the seven-year-long uprising, in which Palestinian youth protested at their treatment at the hands of an oppressive, occupying power, by throwing stones at the armed

Israeli soldiers, posted all over their land. Scenes from places, such as Bethlehem, revealed that life there was very different from the one we had in our heads from childhood. Yet the pictures did not make the deep or lasting impression on us that they should, because they lasted on our screens for only a few minutes, and were gone. The childhood picture of a place of bliss reasserted itself. Besides, there were horror stories of war, famine, and all kinds of suffering from all over the world - some, the result of man's inhumanity to man, others, of natural disasters. We could not take it all in!

The Arab nations, ever since Israel's seizure of power in Palestine in 1948, had repeatedly tried, both by force, and in the United nations, to stop some of Israel's worst excesses and unjust measures against Palestinians, but to no avail. She had a formidable ally, the USA, who had the veto, and was only too apt to use it. There was little help for the Palestinians from the UN. Resolutions were passed, trying to get Israel to stick to agreed borders, but these were never enforced. After the 1967 War, there was more opportunity than ever for Israel to take more and more of Palestine; now she had the West Bank, Gaza, and - her obsession - Jerusalem.

But Palestinians are, at last, succeeding in alerting the international community to *some,* at least, of their grievances. Journalists, who are adept at seeing more than most of us, have begun to present the other side of the picture, the side that was hidden from us for so long. We have begun to get an inkling of the atrocities committed by Israel, in the massacres of villagers and townspeople at the setting up of the State of Israel, of the injustice of forced evictions and seizures of property, of the scandal of Palestinians living in penury in refugee camps, both inside (since Gaza and the West Bank were won from Egypt and Jordan, respectively, in the 1967 War) and outside Israel - whilst everywhere, in what used to be Palestine, Israelis from elsewhere live at ease, on land and in homes for which Palestinians hold Title Deeds, some issued by the British! We are only now beginning to hear of four hundred Arab villages bulldozed, and others turned into kibbutzim. We are very late in coming to awareness of the privations of the Palestinian population in their daily lives - in lack of choices about their lives, in health care, in education, in political, social and economic opportunities, in every way... It has taken a long time for us to start to learn about all the unfairness that has been going on in the land they told us is "holy", but has obviously *unholy* thing going on - and we are shocked to the core. Even then - we do not know the *half*!

Of the tiny areas of Palestine given autonomy - and only after growing international pressure following the Washington and Oslo Agreements of 1992 and 1993 - there is really only one important thing to say, and that is, "The Israelis are just down the road, with their tanks, guns, grenades and bombs." The deviousness of successive Israeli Governments is that they give one story to the outside world, whilst they do the very opposite at home. I witnessed this in 1995, when, after an official said on the 10pm News in English, on January 2nd, that they would not, after all, take the land at Al Khadder, outside Bethlehem, for a Settlement; the Settlers would be given another piece of land (still Palestinian!) nearer Jerusalem. At midnight, the soldiers went on to the land, and shot dead the Palestinans guarding it, and at 8am on January 3rd, the bulldozers were clearing the land for a Settlement! Palestine is further carved up, as roads to Settlements are built, cutting off Palestinian communities from each other. *Their* links are cut off, as Settlement links are established. All this is made possible from the millions of dollars that flow into Israel from the USA, and the supply of arms to maintain an unjust regime.

I have made the point already that, I regard the Christian Church as responsible for all this. Zionism, alone, could not have achieved it, but the Zionism in Christianity made it possible for most of Palestine to be handed over to known terrorists, to do with, more or less, as they pleased..The other side of the same coin is that Christianity is also responsible for the widespread disparagement of the Palestinians. Theologically speaking, since the Canaanites did not matter, all those years ago, the Palestinians do not matter now. I hope that sentence shocks!

The Jewish Liberation Theologian, Professor Marc Ellis, in his lectures, says it is time for the West to stop allowing itself to be morally blackmailed by Israel. He makes the point that Christianity is afraid to criticise anything Israel does, because Israel will scream, "Anti-semitic" and "Holocaust"! Thus Israel gets away with everything. Ellis says Christianity should "end the ecumenical deal, by which it refuses to criticise Israel". And he is right!

But before that, Christianity has to clean up its own act, and rid itself of the war ethic. That means it must get rid of the doctrines of the Chosen People and the Promised Land. This crazy theology must go! The moral blackmail will not stop until Christian doctrine is morally sound, and until it stops equating Israel with God, and Zionism with Heaven.

CHAPTER 13

THE HEALING OF ISRAEL

"Better is one hour of repentance and good deeds in this world that the whole life of the world to come."   (ETHICS OF THE FATHERS)

Repentance is a commendable feature of Judaism, but what if the repentance ignores the main sin? If we only repent of this or that little sin, refusing to call our main sin the crime that it is, what good is that? *None* - it is merely a cosmetic exercise!

In the Old Testament, a Day of Atonement was instituted to deal with the sins of the nation (Leviticus 16). Was it, then, for the *crimes against humanity*, which the genocide of the Canaanites was? No, it was only for unspecified, and even unintentional, sins and crimes against fellow-*Israelites*! It was *not* instituted in respect of the heinous crimes against other nations; neither did it advocate making up for wrong done, atoning in a practical way, where possible - for example, giving back the thing you had stolen. It was ritualistic, only, for the purposes of control by priests, and for the bonding of the nation, and for making them feel very good about themselves, when, really, they had reason to feel *very* bad. It involved the High Priest sprinkling the blood of sacrificed animals, but, in addition to the sacrifices, there was confession of national sin by the priest - but *not* for the gigantic sin against Canaan! The sins of the nation were symbolically transferred to a goat, the "scapegoat", which was then set free, to run off into the desert, presumably to die there of thirst, before hunger or the heat got it. The whole ceremony was deemed to make the people holy (pure), and feel close to God.

Thus, the *true* repentance and atonement needed by the Israelites in the Old Testament to free them from the psychological burden of sin and guilt was bypassed, and, instead of becoming a religion of the heart, became a religion of outward forms, which, far from dealing with the moral needs of the people, *obscured those needs completely*! Spirituality was reckoned to be *obedience through fear*, and to the *gratuitous shedding of innocent blood*. *This* was reckoned to be closeness to God, instead of adherence to the moral code they paid lip-service to. As I demonstrated in Chapter 2, Old Testament religion, even from its earliest days, became divorced from morality, as it systematically *broke* the very moral code it pretended to keep, and turned the religion into concern with outward forms, *not* inward truth.

"To next year in Jerusalem" are the final words of each Passover Feast. The minds of Jews are always focused on Jerusalem. It is the ambition of devout Jews abroad to make a pilgrimage to Jerusalem, especially for a boy's Bar Mitzvah. Those living in and around the city, love to go and pray at the Western Wall. We see them on television, rocking to and fro, as is their style. The Wailing Wall, as it used to be called, was an apt name, for they seem to wail at the Wall.

Why are they wailing? They think it is because of all their suffering throughout history, especially their suffering under Hitler. Yet, long before Hitler, the Jews claimed to be God's "suffering servants". The rabbis see the "Suffering Servant Chapters" of Isaiah (42-53), written in the eighth century BC - not so many years after the infliction of mass-suffering on Canaan - as applying to *Israel*. "*Israel* is God's Suffering Servant", they say, annoyed at Christianity applying the chapters to Jesus. No concern is ever expressed for the suffering Israel *inflicted* - and inflicts - on others!

I suggest *this* is the reason for the wailing of religious Jews at the Wall - a reason they are unconscious of: their own scriptures and their religion violate their God-given moral sense. The record of lies, self-delusion and barbarity is there for them to read, but they will not call immorality "immorality". They refuse to say that the killing of nations for their lands was, and is, wrong. They have a Commandment which says, "Thou shalt not kill", *yet* the whole of their religion and history, recorded in the Bible, is based on killing. I believe that, subconsciously, they are weeping, because their moral sense is outraged. They *need* to confess that the taking of the land of Canaan was wickedness. This deep-seated need clashes with the official religious teaching, which says it was right. There is profound, subconscious guilt. Their spirits are grieved, because they refuse to say wrong is wrong. Their inner being is upset, since their religion has turned morality upside down.

In claiming to give the world the best moral code, they have not lived by its precepts. Sure, they have excuses for doing what they did - the *best* excuse, in fact - God. But we did not believe the Yorkshire Ripper, when he said God told him to murder his victims! We do not believe *any* murderers who say that, nor should we! Why on Earth should we believe a *religion* which makes that claim? It is unthinkable! Yet - the unthinkable has happened - and Christianity has believed it, and taught it, for two thousand years!

Our theologians traditionally said, "The Canaanites were idol-worshippers, so deserved to be killed". We must not be fooled any longer by such (non)reasoning. We must say, "No! Idol-worshippers they may have been, but their religion, with however many idols, must be superior to ours - for their religion did not turn them into murders, but the religion of Moses, and the Christianity of the Middle Ages, did!" Canaan's idols were, therefore, better than Israel's and Christianity's God, if he did *that* to his followers. As for wickedness - it is nowhere shown to be in the Canaanites: they are models of kindness and hospitality, trusting to a fault, altogether lovely - *and they did not deserve to be killed.* Even to *try* to justify such barbarity is wicked! In any event, the *babies* could certainly not be deemed worthy of slaughter. There can be no excuses for that, nor any of it. Oh yes - we have heard the excuses of the alleged sins of Sodom and Gomorrah, till we are blue in the face. We do not believe the allegations. The Sodom and Gomorrah story is malicious propaganda. We know too well the trick of blaming your own sins on others. We see through that excuse. The protest only makes you look *worse*, for murder is still worse than the sins you insinuate - *and you don't even see that*! Pride and arrogance have wiped out conscience. Christians who continue to align themselves with such theology are morally bankrupt!

See how the truth is twisted into a lie, in Joshua 11 v 20: "For it was *God* who hardened their hearts to make war on Israel, so that he might totally destroy them, wiping them out without mercy, as he commanded Moses." What rot! What blasphemy this is! The previous page had just given us a blow by blow account of how the Israelites had emerged from the desert, eaten the very food of the Canaanites for a whole year, then attacked them, city by city. The scriptures themselves show the lie that verse 20 is, for they clearly show that *Israel* made war, not the Canaanites. They only tried to defend themselves. And they were right to do so!

No wonder Jews wail at the Wall. There is deep spiritual sickness there, which will hurt until they deal with it. There will be no peace for them, either outwardly or inwardly, until they acknowledge the truth, repent of their real sins, and work out a new way forward, on a moral basis, with justice for the Palestinians. They need to admit that Abraham was wrong, that God would not do the

76

things they said he did, that they have been deluded. They need to say that their ancestors were wrong to kill the Canaanites. They need to think seriously about the untold suffering they inflicted on others, instead of dwelling forever on their own. They need to learn to empathise with those whom they hurt *with extreme hurt*, ultimate hurt. They need to be sorry, and to say so. They need to get their religion on to a *moral* basis, not the immoral one of hitherto.

It is not that we are guilty of the sins of our ancestors - most of us do not know what our ancestors did, but we *are* guilty of condoning them, if we *do* know, and, instead of condemning them, glory in them. We are responsible for our own views and moral attitudes, and we are wrong, if we fail to condemn wrong. The record of a *huge* amount of wrong is there in the Old Testament. The Jews *know* about it, and, although many individual Jews repudiate a religion based on massacre, the official line still fails to condemn it - hence the deep wailing from within. It is the pain of the knowledge that something is wrong. *It is time to put it right!*

Like Christianity, Judaism needs to put its house in order. They share the same false Old Testament doctrines.
All Bible-based religions need to
1   admit their errors,
2   fix an annual Day of Mourning for the Holocaust on Canaan,
3   encourage expressions of sympathy for the massacred Canaanites,
4   erect monuments, recording their repentance, at the sites of mass-slaughter,
5   help Palestinians to a better life, by providing health care, trauma care, good education, good housing, a sound infrastructure, a sound economy in Palestine, and all other things needful to them,
6   work for the setting up of a Palestinian State, with Jerusalem, that ancient capital of the Jebusites, as the capital of Palestine.
Judaism will have no peace in its collective conscience unless and until it recognises these truths, and takes the appropriate measures of repentance, with amendment of its religious teaching, and of its ways. *Only when it recognises the harm it has done to others,* will it be able to come to terms with its own suffering, for it will then take on a different perspective.

To their credit, many Jews and Israelis sympathise with the Palestinians, and long to have a Government which gives them equal rights, either in Israel, or in a separate Palestine. Some of them have recorded their views in written articles, and in interviews for radio and television. Some also join Palestinians, when they can, in peacful protests against illegal land seizures for more Settlements. They are people of courage, taking a moral stand, which makes them unpopular with their compatriots.

The Jews will no longer need to wail at the Wall, if they repent of the evil done to the Canaanites of old, and to the Palestinians of modern times, and renounce their doctrines of the Chosen People and the Promised Land. They will experience a healing of heart and mind, as they are liberated from the oppressive burden of defending an indefensible attitude to others, an indefensible religion, and an indefensible country. Their spirits will be healed; their distraught rocking to and fro will be stilled. Israel will be able to hold up its head as a moral nation, when it says to the Palestinians, "We are sorry. We have wronged you. What would you like us to do about it?"

Only then can the religion become the moral one its followers *think* it is. - when it repents of the holocaust it inflicted on the peoples of Canaan, calls it wrong, and starts out on a process of putting right the evil consequences of evil deeds.

CHAPTER 14

MORAL CHECKLIST FOR RELIGIONS

"Religions just cause wars."   (Popular belief in Scotland)

Religion, which *should* be such a life-enhancing, peace-promoting force in life - an enormous force for *good* in the world - has, unfortunately, all too often, been used by control freaks, who have found it the most effective means yet discovered for keeping large populations subjugated, doing their bidding. The reason it is so effective is that it has found the means of gaining an individual's, sometimes even a whole nation's, *consent* to being tyrannised. Ancient religions knew this. Modern cults know this, too. In many communities, people, especially women, have no opportunity to make choices about, or have any control over, their personal lives - yet, in the Western world, where most people *can* make choices about their lives, people are often willing to hand over their right to make their own decisions, to others, sometimes a cult leader, who exercises almost absolute control over the lives of cult members.

Moreover, religion should be a source of happiness and comfort, above and beyond other joys and comforts. When friends fail, when tragedy strikes, when injustice triumphs, when death comes - the comfort of belief in a righteous, all loving, merciful God, is a real comfort, which nothing else can give.

It is disastrous, however, to be hoodwinked into false religions, which do not satisfy in these ultimate ways, but which, instead, often wear their misguided and abused devotees out, with strict rules on everything, from what they can eat, and when, to whom they can talk to, or marry, and when, what work they can do, and what money they must hand over to the religion, and so on... All this, of course, is to control the individual; and the record of how dangerous this is, to those who wander, unsuspectingly in, or are born into these dictatorships, is well documented.

To receive devotion, the religion should be worthy of it - otherwise it is a total waste of someone's love, energy, life... But how can we tell whether a religion is worthy?

Science can teach us something worthwhile here - and that is its way of guarding against false theories. This is called "the scientific method". It sets out a proceedure for making sure that scientific theories are as sound as possible, and remain sound, as new evidence comes to light, and new discoveries are made. These are to:

1   observe an event,
2   ask how and why it happened,
3   form a theory,
4   test the theory,
5   note the cases where the theory does not fit,
6   amend the theory, in the light of new evidence.

In order to be accepted as scientifically sound, each theory needs to be tested, and amended as necessary - otherwise, it is shunned by the world of science.

In a similar way, religion needs a checklist to determine *moral* validity, for, if a religion is not built on moral foundations, it is worthless. Indeed, it should be regarded as false, and should not be accorded the esteem of thinking people. Each of us needs to ask ourselves questions about our own religion - questions that will reveal the morality, or otherwise, of our own creed. In my own case, I have been horrified to discover how *immoral* my own religion of Christianity is, when I uncovered the immoral premises on which it is based.

We can ask questions that will reveal the truth or falsity, ie the *moral worth*, of the religion we have been taught. Ask the following questions. The answers should be YES.

1   Is the religion respectful to *all* people and cultures, and disrespectful to none?
2   Does the religion promote freedom, peace and justice for all, and accord every nation the right to exist, and to rule itself?
3   Does the religion accord equal rights to everyone, men and women alike, and insist on each individual's right to make his/her own decisions about his/her life?
4   Does the religion encourage its followers to strive for the life enhancement of *others*, rather than be preoccupied with self and personal "holiness"?
5   Does the religion forbid killing, and denouce war?
6   Does the religion teach a God of love and compassion - a God who heals our bruised spirits, and will, in the end, put wrongs right?

If the religion is not moral, it is not *true*. Unfortunately, the brand of Christianity I was taught, in the Church of Scotland, answered "yes" to most of the *following* questions, rather than the above set.

1   Does the religion depict a harsh God, who delights in punishing, drowned
        animals and people long ago, and sends many to "hell"?

2   Does the religion promote *one* nation, or group, to the detriment of others?

3   Does the religion ever try to justify genocide, murder and human or animal sacrifice?

4   Does the religion foster the dominance of *some* individuals, or classes, or groups, over others, such as male dominance over females, or deny the right of any individual, or class, or group, to make his/her/their own life decisions?

5   Does the religion encourage preoccupation with self, emphasising personal "holiness", whilst it ignores, or accepts the plight of the poor, rather challenge its followers to *help* the poor?

6   Does the religion justify killing and war, on the pretext that these can be "inspired by God", and can therefore be "holy"?

Except for No.5 above, Christianity has traditionally taught this latter kind of religion, which I consider immoral - yet, at the same time, it tries to adhere to the first set! Our theologians will have to do a better job than this, for the two sets of ideals indicated by the questions are mutually exclusive! If you believe the one, you cannot believe the other! If you do, the result is moral confusion, which is the state Christianity is in at present.

Christianity must renounce the Old Covenant with Abraham idea, with its unwholesome sentiments of special blessings and favours for some, and not for others, and its disastrous legacy of genocide, and the immoral glorying of siege and war. The theologians in our Faculties of Divinity can the put their God-given brains to grappling with the problems in the New Testament - in particular, with its relation to the Old Testament, and its uncriticised acceptance in the New.

Spirituality *must* be based on morality. If not, it is a sham. Go to it, professors! Get Christianity on to a *moral* footing!

CHAPTER 15

MILLENNIUM - DON'T CELEBRATE, REPENT!

"But with the woes of sin and strife, the world has suffered long;
Beneath the angel strain have rolled two thousand years of wrong;
And man, at war with man, hears not the love-song that they bring;
O hush the noise, ye men of strife, and hear the angels sing."
(From IT CAME UPON A MIDNIGHT CLEAR by Edmund Hamilton
Sears)

Plans are afoot for celebrations, commemorative constructions and events to mark the passing of the 20th century and the beginning of the 21st. Mention has been made of parties, fireworks, exhibitions, gardens, buildings... and "buckets of booze, and bangers and mash for all". If only it were that simple! If only everyone in the world *could* have a filling meal! I fear that large populations of the world will go on starving, slowly or quickly, to death, whilst others gorge and waste; and some will go on making and trading weapons of destruction, instead of using the finite resources of Earth for peaceful, health-promoting pursuits.

The huge celebration for the new millennium will fall one week after the Church celebrates Christmas, when, once again, the birth story of Jesus is read out in churches, at school services, and on television and radio. Will the message of love be heard *this* time, or will it continue to go unheeded, as it has in the past?

What the secular world, as well as the religious world, *really* needs to do to mark the moving on to the new millennium is *repent of past wrongs*. It needs to renounce the arms trade, war, oppression, and make a firm commitment to *peace with justice*. Then, it would be *worth* celebrating!

The Church should take the lead in a Movement of Repentance. Speaking for itself, it should

1   renounce the false doctrines of the Chosen People and the Promised Land, with their licence-to-kill lie. It should call for the year 2000 to be a year of Repentance for the Church. Two thousand years of wrong are enough! This would be a good start to the millennium, and a good example to others of putting one's house in order. It would put real meaning into the nebulous "Holy Year", called by the Vatican.

2   apologise retrospectively to the Canaanite tribes, whom it has vilified for two thousand years, whose slaughter and suffering it condoned. Alas, there can be no justice, or reparations, for the Canaanites, Philistines and others, wronged so long ago, and for so long, but the Church needs to face up to the unfairness and immorality of what it has taught, and say it was wrong. It must state clearly that *no nation has ever deserved genocide,* and that *God does not inspire war and murder.*

3   apologise to the Palestinian nation for teaching Zionism, which brought about the climate of opinion that treacherously gave away Palestine to others, and enabled Israel to keep hold of what they seized by war, and by terrorist acts, causing the Palestinians immeasurable loss, grief, oppression, suffering and hardship up to the present time. The Church should say clearly that Palestinians are the rightful possessors of Israel/ Palestine. The Church should call for a Palestinian State, with Jerusalem as its capital. Palestinian refugees should be allowed to return to their homeland, if they wish. The Church should try to atone for its past false teaching, by working for the prosperity of Palestine and the Palestinian people, and do all it can to bring about improvement in the economy, health facilities, educational establishments and everything needed by the people for the improvement of their lives.

4   apologise to the other nations of the Middle East - especially to Egypt, Jordan, Lebanon and Syria - for all the devastation, suffering, loss of life, and waste of resources, that have been inflicted on them, through the belligerence of Israel, but which was indirectly and misguidedly, caused by the Church. The Church should do all it can, to make up to those countries for the above-listed loss, by supporting whatever projects of care and rehabilition it can, in their countries.

5   apologise to its *members*, world-wide, for disseminating false teaching among them. The professors in our Divinity Faculties should say to Church members, "We are sorry. We got it wrong. We have taught evil as good, and given God a bad name. We will, in future, be careful to say that murder is wrong, and unrepentant murderers are not holy." Church members should learn from this that they can never blindly accept what is taught, without examining the teaching in the light of conscience. Members should respect their conscience, as a God-given means of recognising right and wrong. They should not disparage this gift.

What the Europeans did, in colonising places all over the world, was wicked - and when it involved, through greed and arrogance, killing the native people, as happened, even to the extent of genocide, in the Americas and in Australia, it is unforgivable. European countries vied with each other to carve up the world under their respective flags, and if they carved up the people, as well, it did not seem to matter to them! They could find justification for what they did in their scriptures, which were rich in tales of the slaughter of innocents.

We cannot undo the past, and ancient history is not our fault - but to keep a wrong attitude about it *is* our fault. To fail to condemn wickedness is wrong. To think it does not matter is also wrong. To express repentance, and to try to put wrongs right for the future, is the only hope for the world to become a better place for *all* its citizens.

It is then up to those who were wronged, to find it in their hearts to accept the apology which is sincerely made, and forgive graciously. A healing process then takes place on both sides. The oppressor begins to feel better inside, and view in a better light, the world outside. A revived conscience floods the heart and mind and spirit with light, in the joy of knowing that right has been reasserted. In the victim, the grief, the hurt, the pain that was unbearable, suddenly becomes bearable, and continues to diminish, as long as he/she keeps a forgiving attitude. The victim who insists on bearing a grudge will never be healed: bitterness destroys the inner being. The only hope for a brighter future for those who have been wronged is to relinquish bitterness, and embrace forgiveness. The crushed, oppressed spirit begins to rise, spreading joy in the heart and mind.

Repentance and apology must be followed by all the practical steps needed to help the wronged victim to a better life, one where equality of treatment, peace and justice are the order of the day.

For the millennium, then, an apology from the Church to the Canaanites, Palestinians and others; a Year of Repentance for the Church; monuments erected which record the Church's sorrow over past wrongs; steps to be taken to right wrongs.

Israel also, should repent of the evil done to the Canaanites, and to the Palestinians, and renounce its claims to be a Chosen People with a Promised Land. It will experience liberation from the oppressive burden of defending an indefensible attitude to others, from defending an indefensible religion, and from defending an indefensible position morally. Its citizens' spirits will be healed, when they are able to hold up their heads, at last, as a moral nation. The nations of the world will come to their rescue, and open their doors, and their hearts to them.

CHAPTER 16

CONCLUSION

"... my mission, to liberate the oppressed and the oppressor both."
LONG WALK TO FREEDOM by Nelson Mandela

Nelson Mandela's autobiography has inspired people the world over, in the beauty of the love and the forgiveness it shows, in the face of the terrible injustices heaped upon the black and coloured population of South Africa, during the years of white domination and Apartheid. The power of this love has amazed the world, for it alone, many believe, averted the blood-bath of civil war that could all too easily have erupted in that land - as it has done in so many other countries, not only in Africa, but in all parts of the world, including Europe, in these last years of the twentieth century. Not that South Africa is violence free - the damage done by the evil of oppression is lasting, and the process of healing, an ongoing one, along with all the normal social and economic problems that other countries, too, are engaged in trying to solve.

At least now, in South Africa, there can be hope for a better future for the whole population. The change from minority rule, imposed by oppression and terror, to majority rule through the ballot box, brought an end to institutionalised injustice, and replaced it with the aim of justice for all. This is the only moral foundation for building any worthwhile social structure.

Judaism and Christianity should take a lesson from this example. They have tried to found moral religions on immorality. *It does not work!* You cannot base a system of justice upon injustice. You cannot found a peaceful future on a system of terrorism and oppression. You cannot base truth upon lies.

We can see the outcomes of attempts to do this on our television screens and in our newspapers - among them, continuing festering discontent in Israel - and in Scotland, people continuing to leave the Church by the thousand each year, feeling it has nothing worthwhile to say. At first glance, these two things may not appear to be linked, but, to my mind, *both* are logical outcomes of institutionalised injustice, and both stem from the unacceptability of Old Testament morality, and the doctrines based on it.

Jesus did not praise Judaism, and it knew it; he rejected many of its laws, calling them "traditions of men", not of God. He took up the cause of those whom it rejected - the Canaanite remnant, the Sinners, the despised-because-they-were-disabled and the despised-because-they-were-foreign.

The Messiah is still awaited in Judaism, to lead the Jews to greatness. What if he should lead them, instead, to *goodness*? How can the past be put right? The same way that wrong can be put right, by *repentance*, which leads to *reform*. There is no other way. The political scene in the Middle East would be transformed. Peace would reign! An example of true morality would be given to the world, and who knows what its rippling effects would be? They could only be beneficial.

As I visualise the outworking of this repentance and reform, I see it as a healing power to all who engage in it - to individuals, and to nations - spreading peace in the world. Christianity *minus the war ethic* could then proclaim "peace to all mankind", in a new way, with a cleansed collective conscience - but it has no moral authority to speak about anything of consequence, unless and until it repents of its own violent doctrines, and violent past.

Then, it is to be hoped, we can all get on, for the *next* two thousand years, in a spirit of brotherly and sisterly love and peace.

REFERENCES

THE BIBLE   KING JAMES VERSION

GOOD NEWS BIBLE   THE BIBLE SOCIETIES & COLLINS

TOUCH THE EARTH   T.C. McLuhan; LITTLE, BROWN & Co. (UK)

IROQUOIS STORIES   THE CROSSING PRESS

LES ANIMAUX MALADES DE LA PESTE   La Fontaine

ALL THAT REMAINS
              Ed.Walid Khalidi, INSTITUTE FOR PALESTINIAN STUDIES,
                                                        Washington, DC
THE BIBLE AND COLONIALISM Michael Prior, CM;
                          SHEFFIELD ACADEMICAL PRESS

THE BIBLE READER'S ENCYCLOPAEDIA & CONCORDANCE
                                                              COLLINS

BLOOD BROTHERS   Elias Chacour; KINGSWAY

WHOSE PROMISED LAND?   Colin Chapman, LION

LONG WALK TO FREEDOM   Nelson Mandela; LITTLE, BROWN & Co. (UK)

A TALE OF TWO CITIES   Charles Dickens; DENT

THE SHAKING OF THE FOUNDATIONS   Paul Tillich; PELICAN

TO A DANCING GOD   Sam Keen; HARPERCOLLINS

PALESTINE - JEWISH, CHRISTIAN AND MUSLIM PERSPECTIVES,
               Lecture by Marc Ellis, May 1998, at the invitation of the
                              SCOTTISH PALESTINIAN FORUM

ORDERING

For further copies of the Great Con, or others in this series
ask at your local bookstore, or write to:
MARION BOOKS
P.O. Box 28207
EDINBURGH
EH9 1WL

POST & PACKING

Please add 60p for the first book ordered
and 30p for each additional bookordered.
Up to a maximum of £3.00 for U.K. orders.

For overseas orders,
add £1.00 per copy for Europe and £2.00 for elsewhere.

PAYMENT

Make all cheques, postal orders etc, payable to: MARION BOOKS
For credit cards:

Card Type:...

Card Number: ☐☐☐☐ ☐☐☐☐ ☐☐☐☐ ☐☐☐☐

Expiry Date:..

Signature:..

For your postal address - PLEASE USE BLOCK CAPITALS

Name:..

Address:..

....

....

....

Note: Book Title ordered:..